Introducing Italian Americana

Generalities on Literature and Film
a bilingual forum

Fred Gardaphé
Paolo Giordano
Anthony Julian Tamburri

Bordighera Press

Library of Congress Cataloguing-in-Publication Data

Gardaphe, Fred L.
Introducing Italian Americana : generalities on literature and film : a bilingual forum / Fred Gardaphé, Paolo Giordano, Anthony Julian Tamburri.
p. cm. -- (VIA folios ; 40)
Essays presented in English and Italian.
"The essays in this volume originate from a symposium held at Florida Atlantic University, dedicated to the integration of the Advanced Placement exam with the teaching of Italian language and culture."
ISBN 1-884419-80-1 (alk. paper)
1. American literature--Italian American authors--History and criticism--Congresses. 2. Italian American literature--History and criticism--Congresses. 3. Italian Americans in literature--Congresses. 4. Italian Americans in motion pictures--Congresses. 5. Italian Americans--Intellectual life--Congresses. 6. Italian American arts--Congresses. I. Giordano, Paolo. II. Tamburri, Anthony Julian. III. Title.

PS153.I8G365 2006
810.9'851073--dc22

2006049895

Cover art: *Reading for Tomorrow!*

Printed in the United States.

Published by
BORDIGHERA PRESS
John D. Calandra Italian American Institute
25 W. 43rd Street, 17th Floor
New York, NY 10036

VIA FOLIOS 40
1-884419-80-1

Preface

THe essays in this volume originate from a symposium held at Florida Atlantic University, dedicated to the integration of the Advanced Placement exam with the teaching of Italian language and culture. The two-day symposium was organized, in part, by the Italian Studies Program, under the direction of Dr. Myriam Swennen Ruthenberg, chair of the Department of Languages, Linguistics, and Comparative Literature.

The first evening of the two-day event was dedicated to the Italian/American culture, whereas the second day consisted of a general workshop on the teaching of Italian in high school and how we might also prepare students for the recently developed AP exam. The workshop was organized and led by Rosa Bellino Giordano, who is part of ETS's team of specialists in Italian language teaching.

The two-day symposium was sponsored, in part, by the Italian Consulate of Miami and a generous grant from the Italian government, and we think all those who made this possible, especially the Honorable Gianfranco Colognato, Consul General of Italy, and Dr. Giuseppe Tiradritti, Education Director of the Italian Consulate of Miami.

Of course, all of what we do in the Dorothy F. Schmidt College of Arts and Letters is always generously sponsored by the Dean's office, under the stewardship of Dr. William Covino, Dean.

Two of the three essays herein were translated by Chiara Mazzucchelli (Fred Gardaphé's "From the Old

Country to the Old Neighborhood: Creating Italian American Literature") and Alessandra Senzani (Anthony Julian Tamburri's "Italian Americans and the Movies").

Bordighera Press is dedicated to the diffusion of Italian and Italian/American culture, and we thank all of the above for their support in making this volume possible.

Fred Gardaphé
Paolo A. Giordano
Anthony Julian Tamburri
Editors, Bordighera Press

Table of Contents

From the Old Country to the Old Neighborhood
Creating Italian American Literature

Fred Gardaphé
SUNY at Stony Brook

Have you ever wondered why most people know very little, if anything at all, about Italian American literature? One answer I found lies in the fact that until recently, Italian/American culture has not depended on a literary tradition for a sense of cultural survival. In my little Italy, stories, never died. As long as a good memory was nearby, the past could always speak to the present. Oral traditions were kept alive through regular and ritual interaction among families and friends. Even though my father died when I was young, there was never a lack of people in my neighborhood who, over a beef sandwich, an Italian ice, or a glass of someone's homemade wine, could tell me stories that made him live again. But as the years went on, the old neighborhood changed. Whole families moved away and with them went the stories. As long as that oral system operated, the need for reading and writing was limited. When that system started breaking down I started looking for the writers.

I learned that the first Italian/American writers were immigrants who learned English and responded to their experience in America through poetry and prose more often than not found in the early Italian language newspapers. While these poets have yet to be documented historically, the most significant work was done by labor activist Arturo Giovannitti, whose participation in the great 1912 strike in Lawrence, Mass., landed him and Joe Ettor, president of the International Workers of the World, in jail. As a worker-poet, Giovannitti edited political and literary magazines. His first collection of poetry, *Arrows in the Gale* (1914), was introduced by Helen Keller. Through Giovannitti, I was able to hear the voices of hundreds of thousands of Italian immigrants who worked their way into status as Americans.

Pascal D'Angelo, who could have been my grandfather, recorded his struggle to become an American poet in his autobiography, *Son of Italy* (1924). To Americans, as D'Angelo wrote, "I was a poor laborer – a dago, a wop or some such creature." That a ditch digger could become a poet was beyond belief for most American readers of the time. Accounts of entering America and facing new challenges for survival became the primary subjects of other early autobiographies such as Constantine Panunzio's *The Soul of An Immigrant* (1921) and as-told-to autobiographies such as *Rosa, the Story of an Immigrant* (1970). Through these works, I so understood my grandparents that, while they were dead, I felt I had to make up for the ignorance I had about their lives. I began interviewing surviving immigrants, most of whom lived in Villa Scalabrini, a local home for Italian aged. One woman was in tears after she read a story I did about her. She told me: "Grazie, sonny boy. Thank you for saving my life in these words. Now nobuddy is gonna forget me."

But it wasn't until I began to submit my own writing to publications that I realized that disseminating my work would demand political action. All the reading I had done told me that my story could not only be written, but that it had to be written. The reading I had done became the foundation upon which I would build my own career as a writer.

At the base of that foundation was Pietro di Donato, whose first story, *Christ in Concrete,* which dramatized the early death of his father in a construction accident, had grown into a novel of the same name, and became the main selection of the Book of the Month Club, chosen over John Steinbeck's *Grapes of Wrath.* I learned that di Donato had never intended to be a writer, but the novel's success placed him in a national spotlight. Published during a time when the worker-writer was often posed as an American hero, di Donato's novel has remained conspicuously absent in critical studies of American literature. Through his novel, I better understood what happened to me after my father was killed, and how I, at the age of 10, had suddenly become the man in the house.

In John Fante I found the Italian/American Hemingway. He wanted to be a writer so badly that he sent stories, accompanied by long letters to H. L. Mencken, then one of the leading voices of American literature. Mencken rejected the stories and published the letters. By 1940, Fante had already published half of his lifetime production of short stories in national magazines such as *The American Mercury, The Atlantic Monthly, Harper's Bazaar* and *Scribner's Magazine,* and had also published two novels and a collection of his stories (*Dago Red,* 1940). His four-book saga of Arturo Bandini, of which *Wait Until Spring, Bandini!* is the first, follows a young Italian Catholic who lights out for California with the intent of escaping his family and its ethnicity by becoming a writer. All of Fante's work spoke to me with a voice that drowned out all the American literature I had read in school.

When I discovered Jerre Mangione's *Mount Allegro* (1943) I decided I had to meet him and to see if I could get him to read my novel. I ran into him at an American Italian Historical Association (AIHA) conference, and got him to agree to read some of my work. As he was leaving the hotel with his suitcase in hand, I pulled out a 500-page manuscript that I stuffed into his already over-packed suitcase against his shocked protest. Mangione, one of the most celebrated Italian/American writers, took the work and later gave me the most solid criticism I had ever received. Years later, the Library of Congress honored his career with a special exhibit, and I have become his literary executor. His first book, *Mount Allegro* is the first of four non-fictional books. The others *Reunion in Sicily* (1950), *A Passion for Sicilians* (1968), and *An Ethnic at Large* (1978), represent stages of his identity development, from Sicilian, to American, and eventually to Sicilian-American. He has also published two novels: *The Ship and the Flame* (1948) which deals with the issues of pre-World War II European refugees, and *Night Search* (1965), a mystery surrounding the murder of labor activist and publisher Carlo Tresca, and *Life Sentences for Everyone,* which contains an array of one-sentence stories, a genre which Mangione invented.

When I found Mari Tomasi's *Deep Grow the Roots* (1940) and *Like Lesser Gods* (1949), I read, for the first time a work by an Italian/American woman. Her realistic portrayal of the plight of immigrant granite workers in Barre, Vt., made me realize why my grandfather had taken so much pride in his menial work. Through Tomasi, Julia Savarese, *The Weak and the Strong,* (1952) and Marion Benasutti *No*

Steady Job for Papa (1966), I better understood my own family's struggle to survive immigration and the Great Depression.

All this reading inspired me to try my hand at writing. My first attempt was a novel that received mixed reactions from a number of editors. One suggested that I follow in Puzo's footsteps and heighten the Mafia material that he was certain was lurking under the surface of my story; another suggested that I change the characters' ethnicity because Italian Americans do not read and so could not be counted on to buy the book, and because Italian/American characters could even alienate those who did buy books, unless of course I was willing to tell more about the many murders that occurred in my family's past. Not willing to follow any of these suggestions, I put aside my fiction thinking that before I could do anything with my novel, I had to change the mistaken notions of those editors. I believed that if I could prove there was Italian/American literature beyond Mafia stories, and that it did not depend on a distinctive Italian/American audience, then my own writing would have a tradition and I a place in it.

From my studies in American literature, I had learned that a tradition is built when writers read each other and learn to either extend or escape what has come before. This process requires literary models, something Italian Americans such as Louise DeSalvo could not find. As she tells us in her memoir *Vertigo* (1996), "Though I had read scores of books, not one had been written by an Italian/American woman. I had no role model among the women of my background to urge me on." For DeSalvo, and other Italian Americans born in the 1940s, a sense of Italian/American culture and identity would come from one's family and perhaps one's neighborhood, but certainly not from school. Without Italian/American models in educational institutions, those, like De-Salvo who would choose to become teachers and writers, would need to look elsewhere. This need for artistic and intellectual predecessors is not peculiar to the Italian/American community. As Alice Walker wrote in her essay, "Saving the Life That is Your Own:" "The absence of models, in literature as in life, . . . is an occupational hazard for the artist, simply because models in art, in behavior, in growth of spirit and intellect – even if rejected – enrich and enlarge one's view of existence." And this is what these writers did for me; they enlarged my view of existence as an American of Italian descent. Toward the end of this essay, Walker writes: "It is, in the end, the saving of lives that we writers are about. Whether we are 'minority' writers or 'majority.' It is simply in our power to do this."

Italian/American writers had saved my life by lifting my eyes to the horizons that lie beyond my neighborhood. They had given me a new respect for my culture, but more than anything, all this reading extended my family. In the poets, John Ciardi, Felix Stefanile, and Joseph Tusiani, I found artists who could have been my uncles. Ciardi's life work has done more to popularize poetry than perhaps any other American. As poetry editor of the *Saturday Review*, he became one of the first Italian Americans to obtain a prominent position as a gatekeeper of American literature. Joseph Tusiani, also a translator, was the first Italian American to be named vice president of the Poetry Society of America, a position he held from 1956 to 1968. The alienation of the immigrant that was dramatized in di Donato and Fante were crystallized in Tusiani's verse. In his "Song of the Bicentennial," written in celebration of America's 200th birthday, Tusiani, raises the issue of the immigrant self divided in the lines: "Then, who will solve this riddle of my day?/ Two languages, two lands, perhaps two souls/ Am I a man or two strange halves of one?" Stefanile, who with his wife Selma founded *Sparrow*, a journal of poetry that they continue to publish today, has translated Italian poetry into English and has contributed essays and criticism to national publications. His poetry, *The Dance at St. Gabriel's* (1995), is sophisticated and beautiful as the best in America.

Helen Barolini's *Umbertina* (1979) helped me to understand the women in my family. The novel tells the story of four generations of Italian/American women focusing on the immigrant matriarchal grandmother, her granddaughter and her great-granddaughter. At most of my family's gatherings, the men would gather in one spot and the women in the other, and Barolini's *The Dream Book: An Anthology of Writings by Italian American Women* (1985) helped me to better understand why women would shift into Italian whenever I would drift near their side of the room. The anthology, by winning an American Book Award, was proof that the rest of the world was beginning to take Italian/American literature seriously.

Joseph Papaleo's two novels, *All the Comforts* (1967) and *Out of Place* (1970) which both deal with the struggle of the second-generation of Italian American to find a respectable place in American society, helped me to understand the passionate life my father led. And when I found Ben Morreale's novels *The Seventh Saracen* (1959) and *A Few Virtuous Men,*

(1973) I learned about Sicily and what it is like to live on the other side of the Mafia. In *Monday Tuesday Never Come Sunday* (1977) he recounts 1930s life in a New York Little Italy that defies cinematic stereotypes. And his latest novel, *The Loss of the Miraculous* (1997), spins a tale of love, art, and loss through an old Sicilian painter. Josephine Gattuso Hendin's *The Right Thing to Do*, (1986) which won an American Book Award, is a powerful account of the relationship between an old world father and a new world daughter. Hendin helped me understand the story my mother tells of how she had once followed her brother across the railroad tracks, and as punishment my grandfather tied her to a chair in the basement for a while.

At the poetic foundation of my own rebellion in the 1960s, there were a number of Italian Americans, including Lawrence Ferlinghetti, Gregory Corso, and Diane di Prima, who had a profound effect on America's poetry scene through the infamous Beat period of the early 1950s. Di Prima's autobiography *Memoirs of a Beatnik* (1969) and her forthcoming memoir, *Recollections of My Life as a Woman*, taught me that Italian/American women can break the hold of patriarchy. This struggle, recounted in the poetry of Maria Mazziotti Gillan (*Where I Come From*, 1995), and Daniela Gioseffi (*Word Wounds and Water Flowers*, 1995), made me realize that the world of my aunts was different from what I had thought.

In college I learned that the way to tell if a literature is growing is the arrival of serious humor and parody. I found the most eloquent tragi-comical Italian/American fiction in *Valentino and the Great Italians, According to Anthony Valerio*. Anthony Valerio elevated Bensonhurst Joes and Josephines, as easily (and as wittily) as he leveled the stature of such household names as Enrico Caruso, Frank Sinatra, and Joe Dimaggio. His earlier fiction in *The Mediterranean Runs Through Brooklyn* (1982) established him as a major voice of Italian/American culture, but his latest work, *Black Italian* and *Conversation with Johnny* will turn Italian America upside down.

What Mario Puzo romanticized in *The Godfather* (1969), what Gay Talese historicized in *Honor Thy Father* (1971), Giose Rimanelli parodied in *Benedetta in Guysterland* (1994). In my early days, Rimanelli had tended to me as though he was my literary Godfather, guiding me in new directions of reading. His *Benedetta* tells the story of America's flirtatious relationship with Italy and debunks the traditional stereotype of the Italian/American gangster through the love story of Clara "Benedetta Ashfield" and the real-life "mafioso" Joe Adonis. With the power and playfulness of a James Joyce, Rimanelli wrote the novel as he was learning English in the 1970s. Published 24 years later, the novel earned a 1994 American Book Award.

Two writers who are have become like sister and brother to me are Tina DeRosa and Tony Ardizzone. When Tina De Rosa's novel, *Paper Fish*, was first published back in 1980, I must have bought 50 copies to give as gifts. The novel, in some of the most poetic prose to come from the hand of an Italian American, tells the story of a young girl growing up and out of a dying Little Italy. Unfortunately, after the press that first published it went out of business, the novel disappeared from those shelves, surfacing occasionally in used bookstores and in conference conversations. As the years went by I would send copies to editors and publishers hoping that one would see its value and reprint it. When I met Florence Howe of The Feminist Press in 1995, she took my suggestion seriously and *Paper Fish* was resurrected with an important "Afterword" by Edvige Giunta.

Tony Ardizzone, one of the best short story writers around, has been winning literary prizes for years. His *Larabi's Ox: Stories of Morocco*, published in 1993, earned the Milkweed National Fiction Prize, the Chicago Foundation for Literature Award for Fiction, and a Pushcart Prize. His first story collection, *The Evening News*, won the prestigious Flannery O'Connor Award in 1986. His latest story collection, *Taking it Home: Stories from the Neighborhood* (1996) features stories set in Chicago and filled with Italian/American and Catholic themes and characters.

A couple of my cousins are gay and lesbian, and the writings of the Italian/American gay and lesbian communities have taught me much about why my family shows their respect or fear through silence. Theresa Carilli's *Women as Lovers* (1996) and Rachel Guido DeVries's novel *Tender Warriors* (1986) demystified the notion of the stereotypical, happy and warm Italian family. Her poetry, *How to Sing to a Dago* (1995) denies the nostalgia of the immigrant myth through lyric reinventions of what it means to be Italian American. Likewise, the fine novels of the late Robert Ferro, *The Family of Max Desir* (1983), *The Blue Star* (1985), and *Second Son* (1988), explore the complex relationships among gay Italian Americans, their families, and straight and gay communities. Rose Romano, poet, editor, and publisher of Malafemmina Press, presents a more politicized persona through her publications and her own poetry. Besides bringing lesbian issues to the forefront, she has also advocated the Italian/American position in the multi-cultural arena through her books: *Vendetta* (1992) and *The Wop Factor* (1994).

In the late 1980s, I met Anthony Julian Tamburri and Paolo A. Giordano, who share my interest. Together we edited the anthology, *From the Margin: Writings in Italian Americana* (1991), which helped us find more Italian/American writers. Short story collections by Sal La Puma, *The Boys of Bensonhurst*, which won a Flannery O'Connor Award (1987), Mary Bucci Bush, *A Place of Light* (1990), Mary Caponegro's *The Star Cafe* (1990), Agnes Rossi *The Quick* (1992), Anne Calcagno's *Pray for Yourself* (1993), Renee Manfredi *Where Love Leaves Us* (1993), which won an Iowa Short Fiction Award, and Rita Ciresi *Mother Rocket*, which won a 1993 Flannery O'Connor Award, all continue to extend the family and provide evidence that the Italian/American experience is varied and very much capable of reinventing itself. Nowhere is this more obvious than in Mary Jo Bona's *The Voices We Carry* (1994), the first anthology dedicated solely to fiction by Italian/American women. Their counterparts in poetry include, Dana Gioia, *Daily Horoscope*, Thom Tammaro *When the Italians Came to my Hometown*, (1995) and Kim Addonizio, *The Philosopher's Club* (1994) and *Jimmy and Rita* (1996).

As my own career in academia grew, I gained strength through reading Frank Lentricchia's *The Edge of Night*, (1993) and his novellas *Johnny Critelli* and *The Knifemen* (1996), some of among the most daring literary moves to ever come from an Italian American. Marianna DeMarco Torgovnick's 1996 American Book Award-winning *Crossing Ocean Parkway: Readings by an Italian American Daughter* (1994) is an intellectual map of the ups and downs of class and ethnic assimilation. Robert Viscusi's imaginative memoir *Astoria* (1995), which can be read as part novel and part cultural criticism, won an American Book Award and established Viscusi's reputation as one of Italian America's leading writers.

The story of Italian/American literature will never fit the limits of an article, and deserves a multi-volume encyclopedia. Even as I wrote this article, there were poets, playwrights, essayists, short story writers, and novelists, busy creating new works. This power of literature to create identity and community has taken a long time for Italian Americans to realize. Louise De Salvo has written, "It is as simple as this, reading and writing about what I have read have saved my life;" those words could be mine, for not only has reading kept me from becoming a gangster, but it has made me a professor who realizes that if reading can save a life, then it must be true that literature can save a culture.

Select Bibliography

Bona, Mary Jo. *Claiming a Tradition: Italian American Women Writers*. Carbondale, IL: Southern Illinois UP, 1999.

Gardaphè, Fred. *Italian Signs, American Streets: The Evolution of Italian American Narrative*. Durham, NC: Duke University Press, 1996.

Giunta, Edvige. *Writing with An Accent: Contemporary Italian American Women Authors*. New York, NY: Palgrave, 2002.

Tamburri, Anthony Julian. *A Semiotic of Ethnicity: In (Re) Cognition of the Italian/American Writer*. Albany, NY: SUNY, 1998.

Viscusi, Robert. *Buried Caesars, and Other Secrets of Italian American Writing*. Albany, NY: SUNY, 2005.

FROM ITALY TO THE NEW WORLD
ITALIAN WRITERS IN AMERICA*

Paolo A. Giordano
UNIVERSITY OF CENTRAL FLORIDA

"Di tutte le lontananze, l'America è la più vera ed esemplare."
(Mario Soldati, *America Primo Amore,* 33)

"Exile is a slinking beast; it bides its time, without hurry, but it gets you in the end"
(Paolo Valesio, *Italian Poets in America,* 5)

Throughout the twentieth century the myth of America has attracted Italian writers and intellectuals. Some came for short visits and wrote about their travels and perceptions, though limited they may have been; the literary critic Emilio Cecchi's *America amara,* the futurist Fortunato Depero's *Un futurista a New York* (notes published posthumously), Mario Soldati's *America primo amore,* and Goffredo Parise's *Odore d'America* come to mind. Others stayed longer and their impact was more lasting; Giuseppe Prezzolini, Professor of Italian at Columbia University and director of its Casa Italiana, was a missionary of Italian culture and a highly respected intellectual who wrote, among other things, *I trapiantati* (1953), *America in pantofole* (1950), *America con gli stivali* (1954) and an interesting article "America and Italy: Myths and Realities" (*Italian Quarterly,* Spring 1959).

Today, several writers, born and culturally trained in Italy, live in the United States and produce

* Parts of this essay have appeared in other venues.

a substantial amount of poetry and prose both in the Italian language and in the English language. The list is long: Pier Maria Pasinetti, Franco Ferrucci, Joseph Tusiani, Giovanni Cecchetti, Giose Rimanelli, Peter Carravetta, Luigi Fontanella, Paolo Valesio, Luigi Ballerini, Rita Dinale, and Alessandro Carrera are some of the better known names. Through their writing a distinctive American voice in Italian literature, or maybe an Italian voice in American literature is starting to define itself.

On the phenomenon of Italian American culture and its different aspects as manifested through its literature, Paolo Valesio in his article "The Writer Between Two Worlds: Italian Writing in the United States Today," which appeared in the pages of *Differentia* (Spring-Autumn, 1989: 259-276), states the following:

> It is worth keeping in mind a motto from the Medieval Scholastics: *Distingue frequenter.* The confusing codes, registers, genres (be they literary or cultural) often lead to reciprocal misunderstandings. In the case of a community such as those" with a hyphen" (Italo-American, Spanish-American, Afro-American, etc.) the risk is even greater. The danger lies in a growth of pseudo-problems (monstrously mushrooming) that slip into demagoguery. It becomes necessary, therefore, to distinguish between the following:
>
> 1. Not strictly literary autobiographical and memorial texts, whose collection and systematic analysis is, nonetheless, important for a dialectical understanding of the various components of literary history.
> 2. Novels or short stories written in English by members of the Italo-American community, containing predominance of themes that can be considered characterisitc of

> such a community.
> 3. Works by those that I have called writers between two worlds: the Italian expatriates in the United States who write exclusively or largely in Italian. (273)

Valesio's model offers an excellent starting point in trying to navigate through the intricacies of Italian American culture, and through a literature born out of mixed cultural and linguistic referents. For this essay I would like to consider Valesio's third distinction, on those writers that he calls "writers between two worlds," in particular on two writers that I consider exemplary to this category: Joseph Tusiani and Giovanni Cecchetti. Tusiani and Cecchetti, as with the other writers mentioned above, operate in, and from a reality that is "bilingual, bicultural [and] biconceptual" (Hicks, xxv). In the terms of Roland Barthes their artistic perceptions are illuminated from two or more sets of referential codes. "Juxtaposed between multiple cultures" (Hicks, xxiii). These poets create literature that explores, is influenced by, and is sensitive to the different cultural and linguistic referents that help mold it. They are "cultural border writers."

Tusiani, born more than eighty years ago in the town of San Marco in Lamis in the southern Italian region of Puglia, is the emigrant who came to the United States in 1947 at the age of 23, with a University degree in hand, in search of his father, the father who emigrated when Tusiani's mother was pregnant with him, the father he had never seen. In the United States he became a recognized poet in the

English language, receiving many awards for his writing: the Greenwood Prize from the Poetry Society of England (1956-the first time they bestowed this honor upon a poet from the United States), and the Spirit Gold Medal from the Poetry Society of America (1969). Tusiani is internationally known for his translations of Italian classics, among which are *The Complete Poems of Michelangelo,* Torquato Tasso's *Jerusalem Delivered, From Marino to Marinetti,* and the recently published *Dante's Lyric Poems.*

He is the author of three collections of poems in English, *Rind and All, The Fifth Season* and *Gente Mia and Other Poems.* Furthermore, his poems in English have appeared in prestigious journals as *The New Yorker, Yale Review, The Poetry Review,* and *Spirit* among others. Tusiani is also internationally known for his Latin verses. He is the author of four collections of Latin verses: *Melos Cordis, Rosa Rosarum, In Exilio Rerum* and *Confinia lucis et umbrae.* He has also published his Latin verse *Latinitas* (Vatican), *Vita Latina* (France), *Vox Latina* (Germany), and T*he Classical Outlook* (United States). Most recently, he has published his autobiography in three books, *La Parola Difficile, La Parola Nuova,* and *La Parola Antica;* two volumes of poetry, one in his native dialect of the *gargano* region of Italy, *Bronx America,* and one in Italian, *Il ritorno*; and a translation of the English poems of Giuseppe Antonio Borgese. With the now relatively famous verses from "Song of the Bicentennial" (*Gente Mia,* 7) – "Two languages, two lands, perhaps two souls... / Am I a man or two strange halves of one?" – Tusiani perfectly verbalizes the plight of the emigrant/immigrant.

In *Gente Mia and Other Poems,* and in the autobiographical trilogy *La parola Difficile, La Parola Nuo-*

va and *La Parola Antica,* Tusiani, with eloquence and dignity, addresses the experience of immigration to the United States. In these works Tusiani's muse inspires him to examine the major themes that are associated with immigration: the spiritually and psychologically violent act of division from one's family and native land (which is the first experience of the new emigrant), the dreams of the emigrant/immigrant, the prejudice he/she encounters, the process of Americanization, the question of language, the alienation and the realization that the new world is not the "land of hospitality" he/she believed it was.

When the emigrant, after a long and wearisome crossing, arrived at Ellis Island he/she was immediately faced with the first major obstacle of his new American life - a strange language. Tusiani knows, as do most of those who were born in another country, that the emigration odyssey takes many forms. First and foremost, s/he must face and come to terms with the actual, physical separation from the country of birth, and from family and friends. This most evident element of the emigration/immigration process is initially the most traumatic. When the immigrant arrives to the new country, the voyage is not finished. S/he will have to undertake other "voyages" in his/her quest to assimilate into mainstream American culture. The most important of these "voyages" is the linguistic/cultural one. S/he must immediately begin the journey from one language, one of the many Italian dialects, to another, American English. Once this process has begun, the emigrant, whose status now is changing to that of immigrant, begins to lose his/her native language and the ideas and cultural values that that language transmits. In other words, a cultural transformation begins to take place, and s/he begins to lose a part of himself/herself. The question of language, or, rather, loss of language, is of primary importance to our poet when discussing the experience of emigration. Tusiani introduces this argument in "Song of the Bicentennial" by as series of questions:

> Do I regret my origins by speaking
> this language I acquired? Do I renounce,
> by talking now in terms of only dreams,
> the sogni of my childhood? What has changed
> that I had thought unchangeable in me? (5)

Tusiani looks at the language question not only as a sociological problem but also as a spiritual dilemma. The answer to these questions is that something *has* changed and that every phrase, every word uttered in English separates him a little bit more from his roots:

> Now every thought I think, each word I say.
> detaches me a little more from all
> I used to love -

For Tusiani when "sogni" becomes dreams, "cielo" becomes sky, and "mamma" is translated to mother much more transpires than the immigrant's process of Americanization and acculturation. Tusiani is cognizant of the fact that words communicate a plethora of memories, images and emotions; the poet knows that "cielo" elicits mythicized visions of the old world and that "sky" will only remind the immigrant of the ghetto in the immense concrete jungle he now calls home, and that when "mamma" is translated to mother much of what was your life begins to desintegrate is will eventually be lost as the immigrant moves toward assimilation into American life and culture.

> Mother, I even wonder if I am
> the child I was, the little child you knew,
> for you did not expect your little son
> to grow apart from all that was your world..
> Yet of a sudden he was taught to say
> `Mother' for mamma, and for cielo `sky'
> That very day, we lost each other... (5)

Loss of the Italian language is for our poet "a betrayal or denial of his original world - indeed his very origin, his very self." (Tusiani, 153-54)

In the autobiographical trilogy Tusiani once again takes up the problem of language. returns to the question of bilinguism in *La parola antica*, the third volume of the trilogy, and discusses it at length:

> Due lingue. La realtà dello sbarbicamento (uso questo termine per indicare lo sradicamento completo) comporta diversi problemi o traumi, prima di tutto quello di un nuovo linguaggio. Progredendo nell'acquisizione della lingua straniera, si corre il rischio, per ragioni di umana vanità, di ritenere inferiore quella materna? . . .
>
> Non si cade in questo pericolo se il fenomeno del bilinguismo lo si considera non come conquista ma come rinnegamento forzato delle proprie origini e di se stessi. Il bilinguismo, cioè, diventa sinonimo di disintegrata unità familiare, per cui una madre non è più in grado di comprendere il proprio figlio. Dal giorno in cui il figlio dice «Mother» per «mamma» e «sky» per «cielo» , fra madre e figlio c'è già una separazione spirituale che lo studioso di linguistica non può catalogare. Se le parole sono suoni articolati che simboleggiano e comunicano un'idea, il termine «mamma», a differenza di «mother», il nuovo termine acquisito, simboleggia e

> comunica un intero mondo di sentimenti che nessuna espressione straniera può comprendere e rispettare. Abolirlo significa rigettare l'esistenza di una fanciullezza intimamente legata a tutti gli episodi, piccoli e grandi, e a tutte le emozioni, importanti e non importanti, connessi ed ispirati da quell'unica parola. Non assimilazione o americanizzazzione, dunque, ma ambivalenza, un'ambivalenza di pensiero e sentimento, di dubbio e di certezza, di sogno e realtà. (*La parola antica*, 143-144)[1]

The consequence of this transformation is that the immigrant, by expressing himself/herself in the acquired tongue, translates not only the language but his/her very soul , and in that process of translation s/he slowly and unrelentingly begins to change. S/he now has the language and the culture of two lands: "America e Italia; in quale ordine, però? Non dovremmo dire: Italia e America?" (*La parola antica,* 143). Tusiani poses these questions because he believes that the immigrant cannot ever be totally assimilated into his/her adopted culture:

> Posta in termini diversi la domanda è: fino a qual punto l'emigrato può assimilare la nuova lingua e la nuova civiltà, e in che maniera dimenticare e rinnegare se stesso in mezzo alle nuove e impellenti esigenze della sua vita? Anche se la risposta sia priva di validità scientifica, il poeta ci dice che non esiste, e non può esistere, un assorbimento totale, e che non potrà mai esserci un'accettazione totale, cioè *spirituale*, delle tradizioni della nuova terra. (*La parola antica*, 143: emphasis mine)

Tusiani's continuous feeling of "uprootedness" lies primarily within this context of never having fully

[1] Also see "Song of the Bicentennial" in *Gente Mia and Other Poems.*

"spiritually" assimilated into American culture. He expressed it best in his "Song of the Bicentennial:

> Then who will solve this riddle of my day?
> Two languages, two lands, perhaps two souls . . .
> Am I a man or two strange halves of one?

It is precisely the unsolved riddle, and the feeling of being suspended between two worlds, of not belonging, and of navigating between two cultural systems that, I believe, pushes Tusiani to return to Italian, the language of his native land, for his autobiography.

The resolution is his awareness of being suspended between two worlds, his acceptance of his biculturism, for which, instead of seeing himself as not belonging to either one or the other world, he can accept himself has being the man of "two languages, two lands, [. . .] two [socio-cultural] souls." After forty years the riddle has been solved. The questions posed in "Song of the Bicentennial" have now become statements.

Giovanni Cecchetti, born in the town of Pescia in Tuscany, is the expatriate who came to this country right after the World War II and, while developing his poetic voice, went on to become one of the leading scholars of Italian letters in the United States. He developed programs of Italian studies at Tulane University in New Orleans, Stanford University and UCLA. Cecchetti has always written his verses and his prose in Italian; not because of a lack of skill and mastery of the English language, a quick cursus through his critical studies written in English would instantly dismiss such a notion, but because of a never wavering loyalty and devotion to the culture of Italy, and a belief that the only true poetry is written in one's native language. In a short essay, which appeared in the Spring issue of *Forum Italicum* (26.1, 1992), "Sullo scriver poesia," Cecchetti writes the following:

> E la lingua? E' quella in cui si è nati; è la lingua d'un'infanzia trasfigurata, carica di quei sensi che allora sarebbero stati irragiungibili. Nessuno può scrivere poesia in un'altra lingua, sovrapposta e quindi fittizia, che non gli può diventare linguaggio, sebbene ci stia dentro quotidianamente. In questa può scrivere versi, magari dei buoni versi, ma non poesia – la quale non può nascere in chi si trova bloccato nella prigione dell'artificio. Noi che abbiamo avuto un'infanzia in Italia (quell'infanzia che in certo modo include anche l' adolescenza) possiamo scrivere poesia solo in italiano. L'inglese è la lingua della prosa.

Among his many publications one finds critical studies of Leopardi, Verga and Pascoli; *La poesia del Pascoli* (Goliardica, 1954), *Leopardi e Verga* (Firenze: La Nuova italia, 1962), *Il Verga maggiore* (Firenze: La Nuova Italia, 1975), *Giovanni Verga* (Boston: Twayne University, 1978); his trasnslation into English of Giovanni Verga's *Mastro Don Gesualdo* U. of California P, 1984) and Giacomo Leopardi's *Operette Morali / Essays and Dialogues* (U. of California P, 1983); four collections of poetry *Diario nomade* (Padova: Rebellato, 1967), *Impossibile scendere* (Milano; Scheiwiller, 1978), *Nel Cammino dei Monti* (Firenze: Vallecchi, 1981), *Favole Spente*(Venezia: Edizione del Leone [Collana "I Piombi"], 1988); and three volumes of prose, *Il villaggio degli inutili* (Venezia: Rebellato,

1981), *Spuntature e intermezzi* (Pisa: Giardini, 1983), and *La danza nel deserto* (Rebellato, 1985).

Cecchetti made his debut in print in 1967 with the poems of *Diario Nomade,* while is second collection of poetry, *Impossibile scendere* appeared in 1978. These two works were intelligently and favorably discussed by two leading scholars of italian letters residing on the North American continent; Fredi Chiapelli discussed *Diario Nomade* in volume nine of *Forum Italicum,* and in the pages of volume 13 of the same journal Danilo Aguzzi Barbaglia discussed *Impossibile scendere.* In these review essays, Chiapelli and Aguzzi Barbaglia identified exile, memory, the inexorable passage of time, modern man's existential and spiritual battle among alienated and alienating landscapes and occurences as the salient thematic elements in Cecchetti's work. [2]

In considering his last work of prose, *Danza nel deserto,* the thematic elements that Chiapelli and Aguzzi-Barbaglia identified in Cecchetti's first two volumes of poetry, and that Rebecca West put in perspective in her review of *Nel cammino dei Monti,* Cecchetti's third collection of poems, are still present and reinforced by his use of the California desert as stage and frame for the twelve short stories that comprise this volume of 127 pages.[3] Cecchetti has lived on the Pacific coast and on the margins of the California desert for the last thirty years. The stories of *Danza nel deserto,* while echoing Dino Buzzati's *Il deserto dei tartari,* strongly reflect Cecchetti's exper-

---

[2] See Rebecca West's review of Cecchetti's *Cammino dei monti* (Firenze: Vallecchi, 1980) in *Forum Italicum* 15.1 (1981): 102.

[3] The short stories of *Danza nel deserto* are: "Danza nel deserto," "Il telefono," "Il molo," "Il viale dei pirati," "La baia secca," "Le lettere," "Gl'ingessati," "Il castello," "Gl'ingabbiati," "Il cassone," "La macchina dell'aria," and "L'ascensore."

iences of living and working in the American landscape for such a long period of time. The desert for Cecchetti is a metaphor for the solitude, which envelops humanity in contemporary society and the squallor, which that solitude represents. In the desert, nature breaks the boundaries that we consider "normal," that is livable; it seems that the desert "does not comprehend man because man does not comprehend the desert." With the desert as stage and frame these stories acquire a highly surrealistc quality . They portray a world of fantasy were reality is in constant flux and transfiguration, while remaining reality. The stories, as the author himself stated in an interview with Micheal Lettieri,[4] are nothing more than "immagini del mondo in cui viviamo, quasi forme simboliche, ossia forme quasi allegoriche" (123).

The men and women that populate *Danza nel deserto* are indivduals who live in solitude, and the more they try to break the wall of solitude, the stronger and more imprenetrable that wall becomes. *Danza nel deserto* is a book about *communication* or, better yet, the *lack of communication* in contemporary society:

> E' il mondo in cui vivo ancora: un mondo di gente che ride e che piange di là dalle vetrate, che muove serissima le labbra, senza che non ci sia mai un interlocutore. So che tutti cercano parole, dimentichi del nido del grillo canterino, e poi si contentano della risata solitaria o del sussurro di colomba.

In the story "Il telefono," the traveller/narrator of *Danza nel deserto* visits an old school chum who lives

---

[4] Michael Lettieri. "*Danza nel deserto*: intervista a Giovanni Cecchetti." *Ipotesi 80* (giugno, 1989): 123-130.

in a small one room house away from civilization. Inside the small house the traveller sees statues of men and women that are really telephones:

> "Non capisco niente," dissi. M'avvicinai a un uomo con gli occhi tesi.
>
> "Non codesto. E' un ventriloquo. Ha il telefono in pancia; ripete solo quel che dicono i vicini." . . . .
>
> "Prova a parlare con qualcuno," disse; "forse risponde. . . Questo."
>
> M'avvicinai e dissi nel ricevitore: "Come sta?" Mi giunse una risposta monosillabica, un suono agglutinato, come in cinese.
>
> Provai le altre statue; le risposte non cambiarono. A volte i suoni scivolavan via; a volte si gonfiavano in modo da sembrar grida disarticolate da giungla. M'arresi.
>
> "Senti," disse il vecchio compagno di scuola. "Credevo che con un estraneo diventassero normali. Invece ... Da principio cominciarono a farmi degli scherzi. Se dicevo qualcosa in un ricevitore, rispondevan con lunghi discorsi in coreano, in persiano, in armeno . . . o almeno così credevo, perché spesso non riuscivo nemmeno a riconoscer la lingua. . . . Pensai che si fossero abituati a questi scherzi perché li avevo collegati alle linee internazionali. Allora li misi sulla rete nazionale. Peggio che peggio: colpi di tosse, abbai, grida, addirittura canzoncine a boccha chiusa. *Insomma voci, non parole*. . . . C'è da disperarsi. (30-31)

The protagonists of *Danza nel deserto* attempt communication but are constantly frustrated in their attempts, either by their own doing or by events that are outside of their sphere of control. They live as in a dream world. Their need to communicate is so intense that they invent ways of communication. They need to invent ways of communication because they are incapable of communication, as is the case, the author tells us, of contemporary wo/man in general. Why is communication so difficult? Cecchetti offers an answer in the above-mentioned interview with Micheal Lettieri:

> Il mondo che sognano, quello in cui poi finiscono per vivere, a volte è molto insolito, come è sempre il caso dei sogni; e quindi non è percepibile dagli altri. E' percepibile solo da loro stessi, perché gli altri hanno un loro mondo di sogni che è totalmente diverso. Questo spiega perché la comunicazione è così difficile, anzi direi impossibile. E lo è naturalmente non solo per queste persone, ma per tutti gli altri che io non considero. (125)

The theme of the" impossibility of communication" is one that ties a number of Cecchetti's works together. In *Il villaggio degli inutili*, a collection of stories that were written when the author was a young man, 18 or 19 years old, but only recently published, the initial story, "La sporta del viandante," clearly explores the themes of the impossibility of communication among men/women and the continuous flux of reality:

> Ogni tanto aprivo la sporta e ne tiravo fuori una casa o dei brandelli, e mi mettevo a studiarmeli in mano. Non mi ci volle molto ad accorgermi che nella sporta avevo creduto di metter l'infinito, ed invece non avevo depositato altro che una gran quantità di limiti. Continuai lo stesso a raccogliere e conservare. {...}
>
> Però troppe eran le cose che avevo e che dovevo portarmi dietro. Un giorno cominciai a tirar fuori quel che ci avevo messo. Ma tutto era incredibilmente cambiato. Ciò che eraoriginariamente bianco s'era fatto rosso, e viceversa. Le cose azzurre eran diventategrigie. Ma che c'era dentro quella

sporta per causare simili trasformazioni? Non lo mai saputo." (17-18)

The American desert returns as a protagonist in *Nel cammino dei monti*. In the poem titled "Las Vegas" Cecchetti deposits the reader in that most surrealistic of experiences: Las Vegas the city of metal, neon and glass that rises, like the Phoenix out of the Nevada desert: the city where America plays. When faced with this surrealistic sight the poet's agony over the faith of society overwhelms him.

Mi rampolla negli orecchi la vertigine
e cerco l'erba antica d'un presagio

Non ti sorprenda se barcollo sopra un filo di caligine
mentre da fondi fumosi frugo n
mentre da fondi fumosi frugo.
Quasi fossi
sul punto di reimmergermi nel caos.

In un'aria di ruggine cascate
tintinnano nell'atrio, guizzano lumi, s'increspano
manubri — la polvere

intorpidisce le montagne nude. Allora
l'allucinato castello resiste
al bulino del vento e sogna
un naufragio di fango e di fiumi;

Las Vegas is a metaphor for contemporary society, a society that has no foundation, a society built on sand:

Se si stacca una scaglia ecco che crolla
a briciole la rete, e non c'è più nemmeno

un'ampolla opaca al chiodo
                    della parete . . . (43)

Thus the desert is a metaphor for our life and society, and of an emptyness that is within all of us and that we are not able to fill, because modern man, in his quest for happyness and knowledge, has fallen into the abyss of despair and all he can see, according to Cecchetti, is the infertile, arid desert.

A CONCLUSION, OF SORTS

As Paolo Valesio wrote in his introduction to he book *Italian Poets in America,* ““Exile is a slinking beast; it bides its time, without hurry, but it gets you in the end. When all the illusions of moderation and equilibrium and normal routine are gone, we find ourselves face to face with a radical choice" (5). The individual can accept his existential condition as "other," or he can deny this condition and try to assimilate as much as possible in the new reality and "with a constant policing of all his rebellious thoughts, doubts, or bursts of despair – live out his life as an adoptive existence" (Valesio, 5). The two poets that I have briefly touched upon confronted their situation in rdically different ways. Tusiani became known as a poet in English and Latin, who has returned to writing in Italian and in his native dialect to somehow find a solution to his psychological state of being a man divided bewtween two lands and two cultures. But try as he may, all of the years living and working in the United States has had a profound effect on his life and on his work. In the last episode of the *Parola Antica* Tusiani recounts that one day, on an airplane returning from a trip to Italy, he dreams that he finds himself with his mother in a long corridor with many doors illuminated by a bright white light. There is a door at each end of the corridor, one marked "entrance" and the other marked "exit." Tusiani and his mother begin walking toward the door marked exit. When they get to the end of the corridor they realize that now the sign on the door as changed to "entrance," and that the door at the other end of the corridor says "exit":

> Arrivai sotto quella scrittura e lessi «Entrata». Mi voltai e vidi, lì dov'era mia madre la parola «Uscita». ... Rifeci il cammino, ma quando raggiunsi mia madre, in alto, al posto di «Uscita» lessi nuovamente «Entrata». ... E per quaranta volte, affannato, ansioso, con la speranza e la disperazione che mi spingevano e guidavano, corsi da un'estremità all'altra di quell'enorme corridoio... (308)

At that point Tusiani is awakened by the flight attendant announcing their arrival in New York. The book ends with this short paragraph:

> Andando verso il Bronx, nella limousine della Poten (his brother's petroleum company), notai un altro particolare: i tergicristalli, strusciando da destra a sinistra, da sinistra a destra, sembravano dire Entrata-Uscita, Uscita-Entrata, ma non sapevo più che cosa significassero quelle due parole, né a chi fossero rivolte. (310)

A careful reading of the last pages of Tusinai's trilogy suggest that may be the poet has come to an understanding of his condition as other, and it is really very simple. In the motion of the windshield wipers that seemed to say to him Entrance - Exit, Exit - Entrance, Tusiani finally realizes that he is a man suspended between two worlds, that he is a man of two languages and two souls.

For Cecchetti the road was different. Cecchetti's intimate ties with Italian culture, his native culture, and with the American West, his adopted culture aand landscape, make him a most original multifaceted poetic voice in Italian literature. His cultural border crossings produce a literature that captures "both the concrete and the ephemeral nature of the seen world and of lived experience, and concentrates on the struggle of human consciousness to move beyond space and time into an acceptance of the limits of both that might lead to the repatriation of the exiled soul" (West, 98).

For this essay I have limited myself to exploring two of the many roads taken by Italian writes in the United States.

WORKS CITED

Cecchetti, Giovanni. *Diario nomade.* Padova: Rebellato, 1967.

_______. *Impossibile scendere.* Milano; Scheiwiller, 1978.

_______. *Nel Cammino dei Monti.* Firenze: Vallecchi, 1981.

_______. *Il villaggio degli inutili.* Venezia: Rebellato, 1981.

_______. *Danza nel deserto.* Venezia: Rebellato, 1985.

Hicks, D. Emily. *Border Writing The Multidimensional Text.* U. Minnesota P., 1989.

Lettieri, Michael. "*Danza nel deserto*: intervista a Giovanni Cecchetti." *Ipotesi 80* (giugno, 1989): 123-130.

Pavese, Cesare. *Letter.* Torino: Einaudi, 1968

Tamburri, Anthony. Editor's Note to "Poessay VI: Voices from the Italian Diaspora." in *Romance Language Notes* II (1991): 13.

Tusiani, Joseph. *Gente Mia and Other Poems.* Stone PArk, IL: Italian Cultural Center, 1978.

_______. La Parola Antica Autobiografia di un italo-americano. Bari: Schena Editore, 1992.

_______. *La Parola Nuova Autobiografia di un italo-americano.* Bari: Schena Editore, 1991.

______. *La Parola Difficile Autobiografia di un italo-americano.* Bari: Schena Editore, 1988

Valesio, Paolo. "Writer Between Two Worlds: Italian Writing in the United States Today." *Differentia* 3-4 (Spring/Autumn 1989): 259-276.

______. Introduction to *Italian Poets in America* (1993): 5-8.

Valesio, Paolo and Peter Carravetta, eds. *Poesaggio.* Quinto di Treviso: Pagus editore, 1993.

Viscusi, Robert. "*De vulgari eloquentia*: An Approach to the Language of Italian American Fiction." *Yale Italian Studies,* I.3 (1981): 21-38.

West, Rebecca. Review of Cecchetti's *Cammino dei monti* (Firenze: Vallecchi, 1980) in *Forum Italicum* 15.1 (1981): 102.

Italian Americans and the Movies

Anthony Julian Tamburri
Florida Atlantic University

As one rehearses a history of Italians and Italian Americans in three major mediatic forms, what becomes apparent is that Italians and Italian Americans are by no means a lacking entity in cinema, music, or television; nor have they ever been, be it from the perspective of their actual presence or simply their mere representation in films portrayed by others. From the onset of each of these three cultural arenas, Italian Americans have been visible. Be it Rudolph Valentino, Madonna, or Ezio Pinza, Italian Americans have had a conspicuous presence in the movies, in music videos, and on TV, even though, at times, debatable. Indeed, this debate rages on, and, while sympathetic to the cause of Italian anti-defamation, one might very well come to it from different view points. The possibility of a monolithic perspective not being the most constructive of manners to carry forward the debate - if not mitigate it to some extent - has been recently underscored by Jonathan Cavallero, as he points out a curious fact:

> In recent years, groups such as the American Italian Defense Association and the National Italian American Foundation have protested the depiction of Italians in the HBO television series *The Sopranos* (1999-present) while ignoring most contemporary presentations of Italian ethnicity and even applauding the depictions of Italians in television commercials for Ragu, radio advertisements for Sprint PCS, and television programs such as the NBC series *Friends* (1994-present).

> Such choices indicate a double standard on the part of these groups as they disparage the gangster but fail to provide the same degree of scrutiny for non-gangster Italian stereotypes.[1]

We may indeed question some of the more popular "Italian/American" movies and TV shows that seem to populate both the large and small screens and enjoy, even among Italian Americans, a certain privilege among viewers.[2] Cavallero rightfully so mentions *Friends*, a show whose Italian American is not the most ideal of models. A similar question mark might be raised about the ever popular *Everybody Loves Raymond*, in which mother and father, together with their two sons, might be seen to impute a certain amount of buffoonery and *fesseria* to Italian Americans, to continue with Cavallero's intuitive vocabulary.[3]

The fault, nevertheless, if this is the right term, lies not only with the producers and actors of these movies and TV programs. It lies also – might we perhaps say on an equal plane – with the Italian and Italian/American viewing public as well as with the Italian and Italian/American intelligentsia. It is, namely, the responsibility of this second group – the cultural brokers of Italian Americana – to articulate a discourse that is well researched, profoundly rigorous, interrogating of all viewpoints in a respectful

[1] See his "Gangsters, Fessos, Tricksters, and Sopranos: the Historical Roots of Italian American Stereotype Anxiety," *Journal of Popular Film and Television* (Summer 2004): 50-1.

[2] For my use of the slash (/) in place of the hyphen (-), see my *To Hyphenate Or Not To Hyphenate. The Italian/American Writer: An* Other *American* (Montreal: Guernica Editions, 1991).

[3] I would also remind the reader of another TV character whom the majority of the Italian/American community has ignored, Jason Alexander's socially inept character, George Costanza on *Seinfeld*.

and therefore non-dismissive manner, and, lastly, accessible to all. For Italian Americans have to come together as one group – inclusive of all Italian Americans – and plan a rhetorical strategy and ultimately construct, once and for all, as Robert Viscusi has so eloquently articulated, a group narrative.[4] This means including even the so-called *blasphemers* of Italian America such as Francis Ford Coppola and Martin Scorsese, or Mario Puzo, Al Pacino, and Robert DeNiro, just to name a few of those who seem to be left on the margins of courtly Italian America by its mainstream interlocutors.[5]

One might indeed argue that the negative depiction of Italian Americans, which has so irritated a certain percentage of the ethnic group in this past decade especially, has its origins in the early 20th century, specifically at the beginning of the talkies era, if not even earlier. To be sure, silent films such as Edwin Porter's *The Black Hand* (1906) and D. W. Griffith's *The Avenging Conscious* (1914) may figure as early, *good* candidates as the springboard for such stereotyping; the Italian character in this film – played by a non-Italian, as was often the case – is an ill-reputed blackmailer.[6] Themes such a sex, violence, sentimentality, family relations, and the like will seem to dominate the cinema of and about Italian Americans, generating a most contested debate,

---

[4] See Viscusi's excellent essay, "Breaking the Silence: Strategic Imperatives for Italian American Culture," *Voices in Italian Americana* 1.1 (1990): 1-13.

[5] For more on this notion of an inclusive concept of Italian/American cultural studies, I refer the reader to my *A Semiotic of Ethnicity: In (Re)cognition of the Italian/American Writer* (Albany: SUNY P, 1998), chapter 8.

[6] For an acute reading of this early period of United States cinema vis-à-vis the representation of the Italian, see Ilaria Serra's excellent study, *Immagini di un Immaginario: L"emigrazione Italiana negli Stati Uniti fra I Due Secoli (1890-1924)* (Verona, Italy: CIERRE, 1997), especially 102-59.

within the Italian/American community at the end of the 20th century about the portrayal of Italians and Italian Americans in United States media in general. In fact, even in his earlier film, *At The Altar* (1909), Griffith seemed to raise concern within the dominant culture by underscoring, in an apparently positive story-line, sexuality and violence as part of the Italian character. To be sure, both aggressive behavior and sexuality will figure as to components of the Italian and Italian/American character as cinema develops in the United States. Be it the gangster films of the 1930s, which laid the foundation for the violent mobster, or the oversexed individuals of the later years, the Italian male will ultimately culminate in a figure such as Tony Soprano, a violent, oversexed capo-regime whose sexual proclivities bring him to the edge of seducing his own nephew's fiancé, Adriana.

During these first years of United States cinema, Italians and Italian Americans seemed to be portrayed by non Italians or Italian Americans. Thomas Ince and Reginald Baker's *The Italian* (1914) is, to be sure, considered one of the best of the silent era. Sensitive to the immigrant's plight, the film follows the trials and tribulations of Beppe Donnetti (portrayed by George Beban) in his unsuccessful search for good fortune and well-being in the United States. Stuck within the immigrant ghetto from which he so longed to escape, he helplessly watches his infant son succumb to disease.[7]

It is not until the arrival of Rudolph Valentino that the presence of an Italian actor in a prominent role can be seen on screen, even though in Valen-

[7] Again I refer to Serra's, *Immagini di un Immaginario* (137-55), for an excellent, detailed reading of this film.

tino's case, one is hard-pressed to find him portraying an Italian in a central role. *The Four Horsemen of the Apocalypse* (1921) and *The Sheik* (1921) were his launching pads and remained his most famous movies. A handsome Italian actor of international fame, he was one of the first sex symbols of the silver screen. Sexually charged, exotic, and rebellious were the characters he played; and in so doing, Valentino the actor may have very well "encapsulated the archetypal Italian in the [non-Italian US] mainstream psyche" as John Paul Russo so aptly stated (227).[8]

The non-Italian representation of the Italian in America continued throughout the 1930s and 1940s, with Mervyn Leroy's *Little Caesar* (1930) planting the seeds for such portrayals.[9] In the meantime, during these same years, directors of Italian descent were most productive in their filmmaking, though the depiction of the Italian in America was indeed slim. These were in fact the boom years for the likes of Frank Capra and Vincent Minnelli, two of the more highly prolific and successful filmmakers in the first half of the twentieth century. Yet, their films rarely portrayed Italians and Italian Americans, an explanation, one might presume, as to why they had the success they did. In having opted not to deal with their own heritage, they may have avoided dealing with issues their audiences preferred not to witness,

---

[8] Let us, of course, not lose the irony in the fact that Valentino's career was launched off the backs, so to speak, of another group of "others." While he did not portray Italians on the silver screen, he nevertheless took on roles of other exotic males, more precisely the Arab male, yet another Mediterranean – a sort of flip-side of the Italian.

[9] There lies a certain irony in that fact that fifteen years later Mervyn Leroy will direct the small film, *The House I live In* (1945), which stars Frank Sinatra and speaks to relisgous persecution, indeed not far of from ethinc stereotyping. For more on this film, see my "Frank Sinatra and Notions of 'Tolerance': *The House I Live In,*" forthcoming.

the struggling life of the working class immigrant or his/her first-generation progeny. Movies with happy endings and musicals seemed to be the choice of the crowd, themes that would have readily trumped thematics that would have dealt with the trials and tribulations of the working class. One might search for secondary characters in their films, but they are hard to find. Mr. Martini in *It's a Wonderful Life* comes to mind in this regard. Whereas rare, instead, is the full-fledged Italian-based movie that is Capra's *A Hole in the Head*, his fifty-second film, yet his first to deal explicitly with an Italian American.[10]

For Italian Americans to be central characters in the film industry, either on screen or behind the camera, it will take a bit longer. At the end of the 1940s, we find names such as Richard Conte in a non-gangster role; and actress Ida Lupino begins making films, writing and directing five films between 1949 and 1953, before including television as one of her two directorial media. It is not until the 1960s, with the onset of a new positive mind-set vis-à-vis ethnicity that young directors such as Michael Cimino, Francis Ford Coppola, Brian DePalma, Penny Marshall, and Martin Scorsese, to name the more prominent, make their mark, laying the groundwork for those to follow, such as Greg Mottola, Nancy Savoca, Nick Stagliano, Sylvester Stallone, and Stanley Tucci.

In addition to the excellent art of filmmaking represented by this group of "new" Hollywood directors and those who have followed, the thematics of their films is most varied. We find the much discussed

---

[10] For an excellent, detailed reading of this film, see John Paul Russo's essay, "An Unacknowledged Masterpiece: Capra's Italian-American Film," *Screening Ethnicity*, 291-321.

"mafia" thematics in the likes of Coppola (*Godfather I* & *II* [1972/1974]) and Scorsese (*Mean Streets* [1973]), which is then slightly transformed into generalized, organized - if not small-town - crime in others such as De Palma (*Scarface* [1983]), Stallone (*Paradise Alley* [1978]), and Stagliano (*The Florentine* [1999]). From large-scale "godfather" to small-time "crook," the mafia theme has indeed left its mark on the American imaginary vis-à-vis the Italian American. A most debated theme, to be sure, the figure of the Italian as Mafioso, has been a popular one. More than just a criminal, let us not reject the possibility of this figure being, for some, transformed into a counter-cultural icon, one who, while initially part of the down-trodden, can eventually rise to "beat the system," even though the system is a so-called legitimate social structure.[11] This seems to have been the case, to some extent, with Puzo's and Coppola's *Godfather*, the prototype for the modern-day gangster.[12] Don Corleone has, in this sense, beat the system, or so it seems. Coppola, especially, has created a wonderfully rhetorical devise that plays well into

[11] With regard to Italians, let us not ignore that southern Italian fatalism that clearly accompanied the immigrant from Italy to the United States, especially during the first 40 years of Italian emigration. In addition to examples of such skepticism and fatalism that we find in some of the earlier novels - and I would underscore here *Christ in Concrete* (1939) - Carlo Levi's *Christ Stopped at Eboli* (1943) contains a wonderful example of how the so-called legitimate system is seen as one of the many necessary evils humankind must confront, be those evils natural disasters, such as storms, maleria, and other maladies, or institutions such as the Church, Rome, and other social institutions.

[12] Two other essays I would include for "required" reading vis-à-vis *The Godfather* are: Thomas J. Ferraro, "Blood in the Marketplace: The Business of Family in *The Godfather* Narratives," *Ethnic Passages: Literary Immigrants in Twentieth-Century America* (Chicago: U Chicago P, 1993) 18-52, and Marianna De Marco Torgovnick, "*The Godfather* as the World's Most Typical Novel," *Crossing Ocean Parkway: Readings by an Italian American Daughter* (Chicago, U Chicago P, 1994) 109-36.

this primary reading of the film especially. This is, in fact, what Marco Greco saw as the "pasta and mobster crap" that Americans associate as Italian characteristics par excellence.[13] In a spirit that complements to some extent Gardaphè's work on the notion of the gangster *qua* cowboy, we would not err in stating that certain films such as *The Godfather* (1972), *Mean Streets* (1973), and/or *GoodFellas* (1989) may indeed invoke a more intense reading that allows the viewer to grasp more firmly the inner semiotic underpinnings of a text. With brief regard to the three films mentioned above, let us not forget that, in each case, the so-called mob figure was presented as both a physically violent and, often, a sentimentally devoid individual — *in nuce*, a pathetic and despicable human being.

In this regard, then, I would only remind the reader of Don Vito's death in *The Godfather*. While playing with his grandson, Anthony, he feigns being a monster. Besides the initial fear he instills in Anthony, significant in itself, two other important items stand out: 1) This is the last image we have of Don Corleone, as he runs through the tomato plants, first chasing then being chased by his grand-son; 2) As he lie dying, unbeknownst to his grand-son, Anthony begins to spray him with what we can only assume to be insect repellent, if not, given the dramatic date of the scene, DDT. Such a combination of events is too significant to ignore; it is almost as if the future generation – the sign of which is Anthony – here now rebuffs the old world of organized crime.[14] In addi-

---

[13] See his interview in Will Parriniello's documentary, *Little Italy* (1995).

[14] In retrospect, of course, this scene proves most ironic and truly stands out from the perspective of *Godfather III*, where it becomes clear that

tion, we must not forget that the subsequent scenes are those where Michael proves to be the cold-hearted person he truly has become: what follows are the intertwining scenes of the five murders being performed at Michael's command, as he stands in as godfather to his sister's child, the one who will soon be a widow, the killing of his brother-in-law also at Michael's command.[15] This reprehensible individual should surely not be high-lighted in any positive manner in what we might consider the Italian/American cinema; however, the reprehensibility of these mafia individuals is brought to the fore, as we see above, and censorship, when their presence might be deemed necessary in the story-telling, becomes an ironic form of aesthetic bullying.

With the second wave of Italian/American film-makers, the mafia theme begins to dissipate, giving way to other issues apparently more immediate to the aesthetic repertoire of these younger directors. Thus, we are privy to insight into family matters and gender issues, all of which is evident in the films of Marshall, Mottola, Savoca, Tucci, as well as others. Working-class issues and the young woman's plight become fundamental for the early period of Penny Marshall's film direction, whereas Greg Mottola's *Daytrippers* (1996) examines marital relations with Italian Americans as the family backdrop. Nancy Savoca and Stanley Tucci, instead, will confront their Italian American-ness head on. Savoca interrogates old-world values in an Italian/American neighbor-

---

Anthony has totally rebuffed the family business and will do only as he pleases, sing in the opera, despite his father's wishes to the contrary.

[15] As an aside, I would remind the reader of Michael's tie. Throughout *The Godfather*, Michael seems to wear the same time, a striped black, white, and grey tie that is much too reminiscent of the classic funeral director's tie for it to be of casual coincidence.

hood and all it involves (gender, work, us vs. them) in her *True Love* (1989) and *Household Saints* (1993).[16] Tucci, in turn, explores the trials and tribulations of the new immigrant as, in this case, two brothers try to integrate themselves into an immediate post-war United States, in his co-directed *Big Night* (1995).[17]

Among the newer artists, those who have made at least one feature, we need to mention Tom DeCerchio (*Celtic Pride* [1996]), Helen De Michiel (*Tarantella* [1995]), Tony Piccirillo (*The 24th Day* [2004]), and Marylou Tibaldo-Bongiorno (*Little Kings* [2003]), as well as those who are still at the short film stage, MariaRosy Calleri, Joe Greco, and Kim Ragusa. After a *tour de force* debut with his short, *Nunzio's Second Cousin* (1994),[18] DeCerchio debuted on the big screen with his *Celtic Pride,* a film that looks at exaggerated fandom among the working class. Piccirillo's *The 24th Day,* in turn, is a psychological thriller that deals with the notion of individual responsibility for one's own actions. De Michiel and Tibaldo-Bongiorno, instead, focus in on their Italian American-ness: *Tarantella* deals with a young woman's return home for her mother's funeral and her emotional encounter with her Italian heritage; *Little Kings*, in turn, examines the rapport between three brothers as well as their individual relationships with the various wo-

---

[16] For more on Savoca's film, see the following: Edvide Giunta, "The Quest for True Love: Ethnicity in Nancy Savoca's Domestic Film Comedy," *Screening Ethnicity*, 259-75; Gloria Nardini, "Is it *True Love*? or Not? Patterns of Ethnicity and Gender in Nancy Savoca." *Voices in Italian Americana* 2.1 (Spring 1991): 9-17; Edvige Giunta, "Narratives of Loss: Voices of Ethnicity in Agnes Rossi and Nancy Savoca." Special Issue on Italian American Culture. *Canadian Journal of Italian Studies* 19 (1996): 164-83.

[17] For more on Stanley Tucci, see, Anna Camaiti Hostert, "Big Night, Small Days," *Screening Ethnicity*, 249-58.

[18] See my *Italian/American Short Films & Videos: A Semiotic Reading: A Semiotic Reading* (West Lafayette: Purdue UP, 2002) 29-52, for a close reading of DeCerchio's short, *Nunzio's Second Cousin.*

men in their lives. All four directors represent, to a certain degree, a new *visione del mondo* for the new generation of the Italian American. While it is true that we still find the "Mafioso" in such films as Michael Corrente's *Federal Hill* (1994), we do find in this new generation the desire to deal with issues such as gender, sexuality, working-class status, and ethnicity in a much more direct and profound manner, an *ars rhetorica* that is increasingly novel for Italian/American filmmaking.

A number of the directors mentioned above have also been involved in documentary filmmaking. Scorsese's *Italianamerican* (1974), for instance, first comes to mind. Here, what Scorsese has done is sit down with his parents and, in the guise of an afternoon visit for what seems like a Sunday dinner, has them recount their own experiences growing up as children of immigrants in New York's Little Italy. What we have is a combination of Charles and Catherine's story with limited historical clips, all of which helps construct an authentic look at one aspect of Italian Americana. Of the younger generation, Tibaldo-Bongiorno, Calleri, and Ragusa have also made their documentaries. Tibaldo-Bongiorno's *Mother-Tongue: Italian American Sons & Mothers* (1999) shows how a special group of seven Italian/American men relate to their mothers, which includes Martin Scorsese, John Turturro, and Rudy Giuliani among those interviewed. Calleri, in turn, offers a unique "experimental" documentary that discusses, simultaneously, issues of gender, race, and ethnicity as articulated by a series of voice-overs and added songs. Most noteworthy in this regard is Tony DeNonno, who has dedicated his decades-long career primarily to this genre, having secured a number of awards along the way. From his *Part of Your Loving* (1977) to his more recent *Heaven Touches Brooklyn in July* (2004), DeNonno has captured the many facets of Italian Americana, especially as articulated on a daily basis in the Northeast.

While it might be argued that the negative depiction of Italians and Italian Americans has been mitigated to some degree by the new ethnic sensitivity that seems to have its origins in both the Civil Rights of the 1960s and the mega-success of the TV serial *Roots* in the mid-seventies, one might counter such argument by pointing to some of the movies by Coppola and Scorsese – especially *GoodFellas* (1989) and *Godfather III* (1990) – and more recent portrayals such as *The Sopranos* (1999-).

The web-site "Italians (Includes Sicilians)" lists overall 209 shows in which Italians and Italian Americans have appeared either in major or minor roles on television. As with cinema and music videos, the opportunities seem innumerable, the showcasing frequent. But it is the type of portrayal that has now taken on greater significance, and rightfully so; as we have well entered into this age of identity politics and subsequently crossed over the threshold into the twenty-first century, the issue of ethnicity begs numerous questions among which we find, first and foremost: Who can represent the ethnic and what are the boundaries this person should not transgress, if any? The jury, we might say, is surely out on this matter, as it is still out on the matter of the degree of validity of such arguments, since one might indeed resort to the old adage that "bad" publicity is better than no publicity at all, further lending fuel willy-nilly to the ongoing debate.

DAL VECCHIO MONDO AL VECCHIO QUARTIERE

LE ORIGINI DELLA LETTERATURA ITALO/AMERICANA

FRED GARDAPHÈ
SUNY at Stony Brook

Vi siete mai chiesti perché la maggior parte della gente sa poco o addirittura nulla della letteratura italo/americana? Una risposta potrebbe essere che, fino a non molto tempo fa, la cultura italo/americana non dipendeva da una tradizione letteraria per la sua sopravvivenza. Nella Little Italy in cui sono cresciuto, le storie non avevano fine e l'interazione regolare e quasi rituale tra i membri della famiglia e gli amici era sufficiente per tenere viva una tradizione orale fatta di racconti e ricordi, in cui il passato dialogava continuamente con il presente. Nonostante mio padre fosse morto quando io non ero che un bambino, c'era sempre nel mio vecchio quartiere qualcuno che, mangiando un panino, un gelato, o bevendo un bicchiere di vino rosso rigorosamente di casa, mi raccontava storie che lo riportavano nuovamente in vita. Ma col passare degli anni, anche il vecchio quartiere cambiò. Intere famiglie si trasferirono altrove e con loro se ne andarono pure le storie. Finché quella tradizione orale si mantenne ricca e fiorente, non sentivo l'esigenza di leggere e scrivere su quelle esperienze. Quando quel sistema iniziò a vacillare, allora iniziò la mia ricerca degli autori italo/americani.

Imparai innanzitutto che i primi scrittori italo/americani erano immigrati che avevano imparato l'inglese e rispondevano alla loro esperienza in America attraverso la poesia e la prosa pubblicate sui primi quotidiani in italiano apparsi negli Stati Uniti. Fra gli scrittori in attesa di uno studio sistematico, spicca la figura del sindacalista Arturo Giovannitti, la cui partecipazione al grande sciopero di Lawrence in Massachusetts nel 1912 costò la prigione a lui e a Joe Ettor, allora presidente dell'associazione International Workers of the World. Come poeta-operaio, Arturo Giovannitti curò riviste politiche e letterarie. La sua prima raccolta di poesie, *Arrows in the Gale* (1914), fu pubblicata con un'introduzione di Helen Keller. Nei versi di Giovannitti riuscii a sentire le voci di quelle centinaia di migliaia di immigrati italiani che lottavano duramente per inserirsi negli Stati Uniti.

Pascal D'Angelo, che avrebbe potuto essere mio nonno, raccontò la lotta per diventare un poeta americano nella sua autobiografia *Son of Italy* (1924). Per gli americani, scriveva D'Angelo, "non ero che un povero muratore un *dago*, un *wop*, o qualcosa del genere". Per la maggior parte dei lettori americani del tempo, infatti, era impensabile che un manovale potesse diventare poeta. Le prime autobiografie italo/americane ruotano proprio attorno al tema dell'arrivo negli Stati Uniti e delle difficoltà incontrate da immigrati in una nuova terra, come *The Soul of An Immigrant* di Constantine Panunzio, (1924) e l'autobiografia raccontata *Rosa, the Story of an Immigrant* (1970). Grazie a questi lavori, riuscii ad immedesimarmi a tal punto nei miei nonni che, nonostante fossero già morti da un pezzo, sentii il desiderio ed il dovere di sapere di più sulle loro vite. Iniziai così ad intervistare gli immigrati di Villa Scalabrini, una casa di riposo per italiani a Chicago. Una donna scoppiò in lacrime quando finii di leggerle una storia che avevo scritto su di lei: "Grazie, *sonny boy*. Grazie per avermi salvato la vita con le tue parole. Adesso nessuno mi dimenticherà".

Quando iniziai a spedire articoli a diverse riviste, capii che era necessaria un'azione politica efficace. Tutta quella letteratura mi aveva insegnato che non solo la mia storia poteva essere scritta, ma che *doveva* essere scritta, e su di essa ho costruito la mia carriera da scrittore.

Alla base di tutto c'era Pietro di Donato il cui romanzo *Christ in Concrete*, ispirato alla tragica morte del padre in un incidente di lavoro, fu selezionato dal Book of the Month Club, battendo *The Grape of Wrath* di John Steinbeck. Nonostante di Donato non avesse mai sognato di diventare scrittore, con il suo primo romanzo conquistò la ribalta nazionale americana. Pubblicato in un periodo in cui lo scrittore-operaio era considerato un eroe negli Stati Uniti, il romanzo di di Donato è rimasto clamorosamente assente negli studi critici della letteratura americana. Grazie a quel romanzo, fui in grado di capire come l'uccisione di mio padre avesse pesato sulla mia vita, e come all'età di dieci anni ero improvvisamente diventato l'uomo di casa.

John Fante diventò per me l'Hemingway italo/americano. Il suo desiderio di diventare scrittore era talmente forte che Fante prese a spedire le sue storie, accompagnate da lunghe lettere, a H. L. Mencken, una delle voci più influenti nel panorama letterario americano dell'epoca. Mencken, dal canto suo, rifiutò le storie, ma pubblicò le lettere. Nel 1940, Fante aveva già pubblicato metà della sua intera produzione di racconti in riviste a diffusione nazionale quali *The American Mercury*, *The Atlantic Monthly*, *Harper's Bazaar* e *Scribner's Magazine*, e aveva pure pubblicato due romanzi ed una raccolta di racconti (*Dago*

Red, 1940). La saga di Arturo Bandini, in quattro volumi dei quali *Wait Until Spring, Bandini!* è il primo, ripercorre la vita di un giovane cattolico italiano che parte per la California per sfuggire alla propria famiglia ed all'identità italiana con lo scopo di affermarsi come scrittore. I lavori di Fante parlavano con una voce che aveva il potere per me di zittire tutta la letteratura americana che avevo letto a scuola.

Quando scoprii *Mount Allegro* (1943) di Jerre Mangione, decisi che dovevo conoscerlo e convincerlo a leggere il mio romanzo. Lo incontrai per la prima volta alla conferenza dell'American Italian Historical Association (AIHA) e lo persuasi a leggere qualcosa di mio. Quando stava per lasciare l'albergo con la valigia in mano, tirai fuori un manoscritto di 500 pagine e glielo ficcai nella valigia, ignorando le sue proteste. Mangione, uno degli scrittori italo/americani più acclamati, mi diede le critiche più costruttive che io abbia mai ricevuto. Alcuni anni dopo, la Library of Congress rese onore alla sua carriera con una mostra speciale ed io diventai il suo esecutore letterario. I suoi quattro libri, *Mount Allegro, Reunion in Sicily* (1950), *A Passion for Sicilians* (1968) e *An Ethnic at Large* (1978) rappresentano altrettante fasi del suo sviluppo da siciliano ad americano, ed infine siculo/americano. Mangione pubblicò anche due romanzi: *The Ship and the Flame* (1948) che tratta dei problemi degli esuli europei prima della Seconda Guerra Mondiale, e *Night Search* (1965), un giallo sull'assassinio del sindacalista/editore Carlo Tresca; e infine *Life Sentences for Everyone*, una serie di storie composte da una frase, un genere creato da Mangione.

Deep Grow the Roots (1940) e *Like Lesser Gods* (1949) di Mari Tomasi furono i primi romanzi che lessi ad opera di una scrittrice italo/americana. Il suo ritratto realistico delle condizioni dei lavoratori di granito immigrati a Barre, in Vermont, mi aiutò a capire perché mio nonno andava fiero dei suoi lavoretti. Grazie a Mari Tomasi, al romanzo di Julia Savarese *The Weak and the Strong* (1952) e a *No Steady Job for Papa* (1966) di Marion Benasutti, compresi meglio le difficoltà che la mia famiglia aveva affrontato durante la Grande Depressione.

Tutti questi romanzi mi fecero venire voglia di scrivere. Il mio primo esperimento letterario fu un romanzo che suscitò critiche contrastanti fra vari editori. Uno mi suggerì di seguire la scia di Puzo, e di puntare sul tema della Mafia che era sottinteso nel mio romanzo, mentre un altro mi consigliò di cambiare le origine etniche dei miei personaggi perché gli italo/americani non leggono, e non si può quindi sperare che comprino libri. Aggiunse pure che i lettori non-italo/americani non avrebbero potuto riconoscersi nei miei personaggi, a meno che, chiaramente, non avessi intenzione di approfondire la storia dei molti omicidi avvenuti nella mia famiglia. Non volendo seguire nessuno di questi consigli, misi da parte la narrativa, convinto che prima di poter fare qualcosa con il mio romanzo, dovevo innanzitutto cambiare il modo di pensare di questi editori. Ero convinto che se solo avessi potuto dimostrare loro che esisteva una letteratura italo/americana che prescindeva dalle storie di Mafia, e che tale tradizione non dipendeva da un pubblico esclusivamente italo/americano, a quel punto il mio stesso lavoro avrebbe avuto una tradizione, ed io un posto in quella tradizione.

Dai miei studi sulla letteratura americana avevo capito che una tradizione si costruisce quando gli scrittori si leggono a vicenda ed imparano ad estendere o evitare ciò che li ha preceduti. Questo processo richiede dei modelli letterari, modelli che scrittrici italo/americane come Louise DeSalvo non avevano a disposizione. Come la DeSalvo ci racconta in *Vertigo* (1996), "Nonostante avessi letto una montagna di libri, nessuno era stato scritto da una donna italo/americana. Non c'era una donna del mio gruppo etnico alla quale potessi ispirarmi". Per la DeSalvo, così come per altri italo/americani nati negli anni '40, l'identità e la cultura italo/americane si potevano apprendere dalla propria famiglia e persino dal proprio quartiere, ma di certo non a scuola. In mancanza di modelli italo/americani nelle istituzioni scolastiche, quelli che, come la DeSalvo, sceglievano di diventare insegnanti o scrittori erano costretti a cercare altrove. Il bisogno di precedenti artistici ed intellettuali non è limitato alla comunità italo/americana. Nel saggio "Saving the life that is your own" Alice Walker scrive: "l'assenza di modelli, in letteratura come nella vita .... è un rischio occupazionale per l'artista perché sia in campo artistico che in quello comportamentale, i modelli di crescita spirituale ed intellettuale, anche se rifiutati, arricchiscono e aprono gli occhi sul senso della vita". Ed è proprio quello che questi scrittori hanno fatto per me: mi hanno aperto gli occhi sulla mia vita da americano di origini italiane. Verso la fine del suo saggio, la Walker scrive: "in fin dei conti, noi scrittori, sia di culture minoritarie che dominanti, ci dedichiamo a salvare vite. È semplicemente in nostro potere farlo".

Gli scrittori italo/americani mi avevano salvato la vita aiutandomi a guardare più in alto, a sollevare lo sguardo agli orizzonti al di là del mio quartiere. Mi avevano insegnato a rispettare la mia cultura, ma più di tutto, tutte queste letture hanno arricchito la mia vita di presenze che adesso considero come la mia famiglia. I poeti John Ciardi, Felix Stefanile e Joseph Tusiani avrebbero potuto benissimo essere i miei zii. Ciardi ha contribuito, forse più di qualunque altro americano, alla popolarizzazione della poesia, e in qualità di direttore della rivista *Saturday Review* fu uno dei primi italo/americani ad ottenere la posizione importante di custode della letteratura americana. Joseph Tusiani, traduttore oltre che poeta, è stato il primo italo/americano ad essere eletto presidente della Poetry Society of America, una posizione che occupò dal 1956 al 1968. I temi dell'alienazione dell'immigrato trattati in prosa da di Donato e Fante sono sviluppati in versi da Tusiani. Nella sua "Song of the Bicentennial", scritta in occasione del 200esimo anniversario degli Stati Uniti, Tusiani esamina il dilemma dell'identità italo/americana nei versi "Chi risolverà il rompicapo dei miei giorni?/ Due lingue, due terre, forse anche due anime/ sono un uomo o due strane metà di uno?" Stefanile, che assieme alla moglie Selma fondò Sparrow, una rivista di poesia che i due continuano a pubblicare ancora oggi, ha tradotto poesia italiana in inglese ed ha pubblicato saggi critici su pubblicazioni nazionali. La sua poesia *The Dance at St. Gabriel's* (1995) è bella e raffinata come la migliore poesia americana.

Umbertina (1979) di Helen Barolini mi ha aiutato a capire le donne della mia famiglia. Il romanzo racconta le vite di quattro generazioni di donne italo/americane, soffermandosi sulla storia della nonna immigrata, della nipote e della pronipote. *The Dream Book: An Anthology of Writings by Italian American Women* (1985) sempre della Barolini mi ha aiutato a capire perché quando mi avvicinavo per caso al gruppetto di donne nelle riunioni di famiglia, la discussione passava automaticamente dall'inglese all' italiano! Aggiudicandosi l'American Book Award, l' antologia della Barolini dimostrò che il resto del mondo iniziava a prendere la letteratura italo/americana sul serio.

I due romanzi di Joseph Papaleo, *All the Comforts* (1967) e *Out of Place* (1970), che trattano entrambi della lotta di un italo/americano di seconda generazione per trovare un posto di tutto rispetto nella società americana, mi aiutarono a capire cosa aveva dovuto provare mio padre. Dai romanzi di Ben Morreale *The Seventh Saracen* (1959) e *A Few Virtuous Men* (1973) imparai molto sulla Sicilia e su cosa significa vivere dall'altra parte della Mafia. In *Monday Tuesday Never Come Sunday* (1977), Morreale racconta la vita nella Little Italy di New York negli anni '30 in un modo che sfida gli stereotipi cinematografici, mentre il suo ultimo romanzo, *The Loss of the Miraculous* (1997), è una storia d'amore, arte, e perdita raccontata attraverso un pittore siciliano. *The Right Thing to Do* (1986) di Josephine Gattuso Hendin, vincitore di un American Book Award, è un bel resoconto della relazione tra un padre del vecchio mondo ed una figlia del nuovo. La Hendin mi ha aiutato a capire la storia che racconta mia madre di quando una volta, per aver seguito suo fratello al di là della ferrovia, mio nonno la punì legandola ad una sedia nel seminterrato.

Diversi poeti italo/americani ispirarono la mia ribellione negli anni '60, fra cui Lawrence Ferlinghetti, Gregory Corso e Diane di Prima che, in quanto protagonisti del movimento Beat, rivoluzionarono lo scenario poetico americano dei primi anni '50. L'autobiografia della Di Prima *Memoirs of a*

Beatnik (1969) e le sue memorie *Recollections of My Life as a Woman* mi hanno insegnato che le donne italo/americane possono scardinare il sistema patriarcale. E i versi di Maria Mazziotti Gillan (*Where I Come From*, 1995), e Daniela Gioseffi (*Word Wounds and Water Flowers,* 1995) mi aprirono finalmente gli occhi sul fatto che il mondo delle mie zie era molto diverso da come me lo immaginavo.

All'università imparai che bisogna che faccia apparizione l'umorismo e la parodia perché una letteratura possa dirsi matura. L'esempio più eclatante di fiction tragicomica italo/americana è *Valentino and the Great Italians, According to Anthony Valerio.* Anthony Valerio ha reso importanti i Joes e Josephines di Bensonhurst, ridimensionando allo stesso tempo l'aura di mito che circonda i nomi Enrico Caruso, Frank Sinatra e Joe Dimaggio. Il suo primo romanzo *The Mediterranean Runs Through Brooklyn* (1982) ne ha fatto una delle voci più rappresentative della cultura italo/americana; ma saranno soprattutto i suoi ultimi lavori, *Black Italian* e *Conversation with Johnny,* a sconvolgere l'America italiana.

Quello che Mario Puzo ha romanzato ne *Il Padrino* (1969), che Gay Talese ha storicizzato in *Honor Thy Father* (1971), Giose Rimanelli lo ha parodiato in *Benedetta in Guysterland* (1994). All'inizio della mia carriera, Rimanelli mi è stato vicino quasi come un padrino letterario, guidandomi verso nuove direzioni di lettura. *Benedetta* tratta dell'ossessione nutrita dall'America nei confronti della Mafia, e ribalta lo stereotipo del gangster italo/americano attraverso la storia d'amore di Clara "Benedetta Ashfield" ed il vero "mafioso" Joe Adonis. La prima stesura del romanzo, scritto con uno stile degno di James Joyce, risale agli anni '70, quando Rimanelli stava ancora lottando per imparare l'inglese. Pubblicato ventiquattro anni dopo, *Benedetta* vinse l'American Book Award.

Tina DeRosa e Tony Ardizzone diventarono per me un fratello ed una sorella. Quando *Paper Fish* della DeRosa fu pubblicato per la prima volta nel 1980, comprai qualcosa una cinquantina di copie per regalarle ai miei amici. Il romanzo, scritto in una delle prose più poetiche che siano mai venute fuori da una penna italo/americana, racconta la storia di una ragazzina che cresce in una Little Italy che sta per morire. Purtroppo, dopo che la casa editrice che lo pubblicò chiuse i battenti, il romanzo sparì dalla circolazione, riapparendo solo di tanto in tanto fra libri usati e in conversazioni fra specialisti. Nel frattempo io spedivo copie ad editori e stampatori sperando che qualcuno se ne interessasse e lo ripubblicasse. Quando incontrai per la prima volta Florence Howe di *The Feminist Press* nel 1995, questa s'interessò seriamente a *Paper Fish*, ed il romanzo fu finalmente ripubblicato con un'importante postfazione di Edvige Giunta.

Tony Ardizzone, uno dei migliori scrittori moderni di racconti, già da anni colleziona premi letterari. La sua raccolta *Larabi's Ox: Stories of Morocco*, pubblicata nel 1993, ha vinto il Milkweed National Fiction Prize, il Chicago Foundation for Literature Award for Fiction e un Pushcart Prize. La sua prima raccolta di racconti, The *Evening News*, ha vinto il prestigioso Flannery O'Connor Award nel 1986. La sua ultima raccolta, *Taking it Home: Stories from the Neighborhood* (1996) include storie ambientate a Chicago e tratta temi e personaggi italo/americani e cattolici.

La letteratura gay e lesbica italo/americana mi ha insegnato perché la mia famiglia mostra rispetto o paura nei confronti dell'omosessualità di alcuni dei miei cugini attraverso il silenzio. *Women as Lovers* (1996) di Theresa Carilli ed il romanzo di Rachel Guido DeVries *Tender Warriors* (1986) demistificano la nozione della famiglia italiana calda e accogliente. La poesia della DeVries *How to Sing to a Dago* (1995) nega la nostalgia del mito dell'immigrato re-inventando liricamente il significato dell'identità italo/americana. Allo stesso modo, i bei romanzi di Roberto Ferro, *The Family of Max Desir* (1983), *The Blue Star* (1985), e *Second Son* (1988), esplorano il complesso rapporto tra i gay italo/americani, le loro famiglie, e fra le comunità gay ed etero. Rose Romano, poetessa, editrice, e direttrice della Malafemmina Press presenta un'immagine più politicizzata di sé sia nei lavori di critica che in poesia. Oltre ad affrontare pubblicamente tematiche lesbiche, la Romano si è soprattutto fatta sostenitrice della presenza italo/americana nell'arena multiculturale con i libri *Vendetta* (1992) e *The Wop Factor* (1994).

Alla fine degli anni '80 ho conosciuto Anthony Julian Tamburri e Paolo A. Giordano, con i quali condivido l'interesse per la causa della letteratura italo/americana. Insieme abbiamo curato un'antologia, *From the Margin: Writings in Italian Americana* (1991), che ci ha permesso di scovare un maggior numero di scrittori italo/americani. In raccolte di racconti quali *The Boys of Bensonhurst* di Sal La Puma, che ha vinto un Flannery O'Connor Award (1987), *A Place of Light* (1990) di Mary Bucci Bush, *The Star Cafe* (1990) di Mary Caponegro, *The Quick* (1992) di Agnes Rossi, *Pray for Yourself* (1993) di Anne Calcagno, *Where Love Leaves Us* (1993) di Renee Manfredi, che ha vinto uno Iowa Short Fiction Award, e *Mother Rocket* di Rita Ciresi, che ha vinto nel 1993 un Flannery O'Connor Award, le tematiche della famiglia vengono estese e trattate al fine di provare che l'esperienza italo/americana è varia e capace di re-inventarsi. Ciò è soprattutto evidente in *The Voices We Carry* (1994) di Mary Jo Bona, la prima antologia dedicata esclusivamente alla narrativa di scrittrici italo/americane. Nel campo della poesia, degne di nota sono *Daily Horoscope* di Dana Gioia, *When the Italians Came to my Hometown* (1995) di Thom Tammaro, e *The Philosopher's Club* (1994) e *Jimmy and Rita* (1996) di Kim Addonizio.

Mentre la mia carriera all'interno dell'università avanzava, mi sono avvalso della lettura di *The Edge of Night* (1993) di Frank Lentricchia, mentre le sue novelle *Johnny Critelli* e *The Knifemen* (1996) sono alcune delle più coraggiose imprese letterarie ad opera di italo/americani. *Crossing Ocean Parkway: Readings by an Italian American Daughter* (1994) di Marianna DeMarco Torgovnick, vincitore nel 1996 dell'American Book Award, è una mappa intellettuale degli alti e bassi dell'assimilazione etnica e di classe. Il libro di memorie immaginarie di Robert Viscusi, *Astoria* (1995), che può essere letto in parte come romanzo e in parte come critica culturale, si è aggiudicato un American Book Award, e ne ha affermato così la reputazione come uno dei maggiori scrittori italo/americani.

La storia della letteratura italo/american non troverà mai spazio nei limiti angusti di un saggio, e meriterebbe un'enciclopedia a più volumi. Mentre scrivo questo articolo, poeti, drammaturghi, saggisti, scrittori di racconti e romanzi stanno lavorando a qualcosa di nuovo. C'è voluto del tempo perché la letteratura potesse creare un'identità e una comunità fra gli italo/americani. Louise De Salvo ha scritto: "È così: leggere e scrivere su quello che ho letto mi ha salvato la vita". Queste parole potrebbero essere mie, perché non solo la passione per i libri mi ha impedito di diventare un gangster, ma ha fatto di me un professore, convinto che se leggere può salvare una vita, allora deve essere vero che la letteratura può salvare una cultura.

Select Bibliography

Bona, Mary Jo. *Claiming a Tradition: Italian American Women Writers*. Carbondale, IL: Southern Illinois UP, 1999.

Gardaphè, Fred. *Italian Signs, American Streets: The Evolution of Italian American Narrative*. Durham, NC: Duke University Press, 1996

Giunta, Edvige. *Writing with An Accent: Contemporary Italian American Women Authors*. New York, NY: Palgrave, 2002.

Tamburri, Anthony Julian. *A Semiotic of Ethnicity: In (Re) Cognition of the Italian/American Writer*. Albany, NY: SUNY, 1998.

Viscusi, Robert. *Buried Caesars, and Other Secrets of Italian American Writing*. Albany, NY: SUNY, 2005.

Dall'Italia al nuovo mondo
scrittori italiani in America

Paolo A. Giordano
University of Central Florida

"Di tutte le lontananze, l'America è la più vera ed esemplare"
(Mario Soldati, *America primo amore*, 33)

"Exile is a slinking beast; it bides its time, without hurry, but it gets you in the end"
(Paolo Valesio, *Italian Poets in America*, 5)

Per tutto il ventesimo secolo l'immaginazione degli scrittori italiani e degli intellettuali è stata attratta dal mito dell'America. Alcuni sono venuti per brevi visite, hanno scritto del loro viaggio e hanno riportato le loro impressioni, a volte parziali e particolari, frutto di viaggi geograficamente e temporalmente limitati. Penso a *America amara* di Emilio Cecchi, *Un futurista a New York* di Fortunato Depero (pubblicato postumo da appunti dell'artista), *America primo amore* di Mario Soldati, e *Odore d'America* di Goffredo Parise. Altri sono rimasti per un periodo più lungo e il loro impatto è stato più duraturo; l'esempio più rilevante è quello di Giuseppe Prezzolini, professore d'Italiano presso la Columbia University e direttore della Casa Italiana della stessa Università. Missionario della cultura italiana, Prezzolini ha fra le sue numerose pubblicazioni libri che riflettono sulla sua permanenza negli Stati Uniti: *America in pantofole*, *I trapiantati*, *America con gli stivali* e un articolo molto interessante "America and Italy: Myths and Realities" (*Italian Quarterly*, 1959).

Oggi, un numero di scrittori, nati e educati in Italia vivono negli Stati Uniti e esercitano la loro arte sia in lingua italiana sia in lingua inglese. La lista è lunga: Pier Maria Pasinetti, Franco Ferrucci, Joseph Tusiani, Giovanni Cecchetti, Giose Rimanelli, Peter Carravetta, Luigi Fontanella, Paolo Valesio, Luigi Ballerini, Rita Dinale e Alessandro Carrera sono fra i nomi più conosciuti. Attraverso la loro scrittura va formandosi una distinta voce americana nella letteratura italiana (o forse una voce italiana nella letteratura americana). Inoltre, la pubblicazione di due volumi dedicati alla poesia italiana negli Stati Uniti da più credito a questa nuova voce emergente; mi riferisco a *Poeti italiani in America*, un numero speciale di Gradiva International Journal of Italian Literature curata da Luigi Fontanella e Paolo Valesio, e *Poesaggio* curata da Peter Carravetta e Paolo Valesio. Non è mia intenzione, in questo saggio, affrontare in modo critico questi due libri storici per il loro genere. Mi sembra tuttavia importante sottolineare che queste due antologie danno voce alla diaspora italiana negli Stati Uniti, e che dalla loro forma e contenuto ci fanno riconoscere il fatto che la cultura italo-americana non è monolinguistica nè monoculturale.[1]

Sul fenomeno della cultura italiana in America e i suoi diversi aspetti manifestati nella letteratura, Paolo Valesio nel suo articolo "The Writer Between Two Worlds: Italian writing in the United States Today," apparso nelle pagine di *Differentia* (Spring-Autumn, 1989: 259-276), scrive:

[1] Da vedere Anthony Tamburri, "Editor's Note" al "Poessay VI: Voices From the Italian Diaspora" in *Romance Languages Annual II* (1991).

> It is worth keeping in mind a motto from the Medieval Scholastics: *Distingue frequenter.* The confusing codes, registers, genres (be they literary or cultural) often leads to reciprocal misunderstandings. In the case of a community such as those "with a hyphen" (Italo-American, Spanish-American, Afro-American, etc.) the risk is even greater. The danger lies in a growth of pseudo-problems (monstrously mushrooming) that slip into demagoguery. It becomes necessary, therefore, to distinguish between the following:
>
> 1. Not strictly literary autobiographical and memorial texts, whose collection and systematic analysis is, nonetheless, important for a dialectical understanding of the various components of literary history.
> 2. Novels or short stories written in English by members of the Italo-American community, containing predominance of themes that can be considered characterisitc of such a community.
> 3. Works by those that I have called writers between two worlds: the Italian expatriates in the United States who write exclusively or largely in Italian. (273)

Il modello di Valesio offre un eccellente punto di partenza per uno che voglia addentrarsi nella selva della cultura italo americana, e in una letteratura, quella italo americana, nata da referenti multiculturali e multilinguistici.

In questo saggio vorrei soffermarmi sulla teza distinzione che fa il Valesio, cioè quegli scrittori che lui chiama "scrittori fra due mondi," e più specificamente su due scrittori che rappresentano due dei molti percorsi che la scrittura italiana negli Stati Uniti ha intrapreso: Joseph Tusiani e Giovanni Cecchetti. Tusiani e Cecchetti sono scrittori educati nel paese di nascita, in questo caso l'Italia, ma culturalmente e intellettualmente attivi in un altro, in questo caso gli Stati Uniti; essi operano in una realtà che è "bilingue, biculturale e biconcettuale,"(Hicks, xxv) e da questa realtà traggono molto della loro ispirazione. Usando le parole di Roland Barthes, le loro percezioni artistiche sono illuminate da due o più gruppi di codici referenziali. "Sovrapposti fra culture multiple" (Hicks, xxxiii) questi poeti creano una letteratura che esplora, è influenzata, ed è sensibile a diversi referenti culturali e linguistici che aiutano a formarla. Sono scrittori ai confini culturali ("cultural border writers").

Joseph Tusiani nato 71 anni fa in San Marco in Lamis, piccolo paese del Gargano, dopo aver ottenuto la laurea, è emigrato nel 1947 all'età di 23 anni e già laureato, alla ricerca del padre mai conosciuto che era partito quando la mamma di Tusiani era incinta di lui. Negli Stati Uniti è diventato poeta in lingua inglese, e ha ricevuto molti riconoscimenti per il suo lavoro: il Greewood Prize dalla Poetry Society of England nel 1956l e la Spirit Gold Medal dalla Poetry Society of America nel 1969. Profiquo scrittore, ha pubblicato varie raccolte di versi in inglese, fra le quali *Rind and All, The Fifth Season,* e *Gente Mia and Other Poems*; è autore di quattro raccolte di poesie in latino: *Melos Cordis, Rosa Rosarum, In Exilio Rerum* e *Confinia lucis et umbrae* e numerose raccolte di poesie nel dialetto del Gargano. Una autobiografia in tre volumi, *La parola difficile, La parola nuova,* e *La parola antica.*

Con *Gente mia and other poems* e la trilogia autobiografica, Tusiani, con eloquenza e dignità, si rivolge al fenomeno dell'emigrazione italiana negli Stati Uniti. In queste opere egli esamina i temi principali che riguardano l'emigrazione: il gesto spiritualmente e psicologicamente violento della divisione dalla famiglia e dalla terra natia (cioè la prima esperienza del nuovo emigrante), i sogni dell'emigrante, i pregiudizi che incontra, il processo di americanizzazzione, la questione (o meglio il problema) della lingua, l'alienazione e l'accorgersi che il nuovo mondo non è la terra dell'ospitalità da lui/lei creduta.

Quando l'emigrante dopo una lunga, tortuosa, e stancante traversata oceanica arriva a Ellis Island, si trova di fronte all'ostacolo maggiore della sua nuova realtà americana – la lingua inglese. Tusiani sa, come la maggior parte di coloro che sono nati in un altro paese, che l'odissea dell' emigrazione è piena di pericoli. Il primo e più importante di questi ostacoli che l'emigrante deve affrontare è la separazione fisica dal paese di nascita, dalla famiglia e dagli amici. Questo aspetto, il più evidente del processo dell'emigrazione, è inizialmente il più traumatico. Quando l'emigrante arriva nel paese di destinazione presto si accorge che il suo viaggio non è finito e che deve intraprendere altri "viaggi" nella sua ricerca di assimilazione della cultura dominante (cioè quella americana). Il più importante di questi "viaggi" è quello linguistico culturale. L'emigrante deve immediatamente iniziare il viaggio da una lingua, normalmente il dialetto del paese, all'altra, l'inglese americano. Una volta iniziato questo processo l'emigrante, la cui posizione sociale sta cambiando da emigrante a immigrante, comincia a perdere la sua lingua natia e le idee e i valori culturali che quella lingua trasmette. Ha luogo una trasformazione culturale e l'immigrante inizia a perdere una parte di sé. La questione della lingua, o meglio la perdita della lingua, è di primaria importanza per Tusiani. Tusiani presenta il suo punto di vista in "Song of the Bicentennial" (Canzone del bicentenario), prima composizione di *Gente Mia and Other Poems*, con una serie di domande:

> Do I regret my origins by speaking
> this language I acquired? Do I renounce,
> by talking now in terms of only dreams,
> the sogni of my childhood? What has changed
> that I had thought unchangeable in me? (5)

Tusiani guarda al problema della lingua non solo come un problema sociologico, ma anche come un dilemma spirituale. La risposta a queste domande è che qualcosa è cambiato e che ogni frase, ogni parola pronunciata in inglese lo separa sempre più dalle sue radici:

> Now every thought I think, each word I say
> detaches me a little more from all
> I used to love.

Quando nei versi di Tusiani sogni diventano "dreams," cielo diventa "sky" e mamma diventa "mother" si può cogliere molto di più del semplice processo di americanizazzione e di acculturazione dell'immigrante. Tusiani è cosciente del fatto che le parole comunicano una molteplicità di memorie, immagini ed emozioni; il poeta sa che per l'immigrante la parola "cielo" sprigiona visioni mitiche del vecchio mondo e che invece "sky" ricorda il ghetto nella immensa giungla di cemento, cioè la metropoli americana, che adesso lui/lei chiama casa, e che quando "mamma" viene tradotto in "mother" molto di ciò che era la sua vita comincia a disintegrarsi e verrà perduto man mano che l'immigrante si muove assimilato, nella vita e nella cultura americana.

Mother, I even wonder if I am
the child I was, the little child you knew,
for you did not expect your little son
to grow apart from all that was your world.
Yet of a sudden he was taught to say
'Mother' for mamma, and for cielo 'sky'
That very day, we lost each other... (5)

Per il nostro poeta la perdita della lingua italiana è un tradimento e un rigetto del mondo di origine – delle sue origini, e del suo essere.

Nella trilogia autobiografica Tusiani riprende il problema della lingua. Rivisita la questione del bilinguismo nel volume la *La parola antica*, il terzo della trilogia e ne discutre ampiamente:

> Due lingue. La realtà dello sbarbicamento (uso questo termine per indicare lo sradicamento completo) comporta diversi problemi o traumi, prima di tutto quello di un nuovo linguaggio. Progredendo nell'acquisizione della lingua straniera, si corre il rischio, per ragioni di umana vanità, di ritenere inferiore quella materna? [...]
>
> Non si cade in questo pericolo se il fenomeno del bilinguismo lo si considera non come conquista ma come rinnegamento forzato delle proprie origini e di se stessi. Il bilinguismo, cioè, diventa sinonimo di disintegrata unità familiare, per cui una madre non è più in grado di comprendere il proprio figlio. Dal giorno in cui il figlio dice «Mother» per «mamma» e «sky» per «cielo», fra madre e figlio c'è già una separazione spirituale che lo studioso di linguistica non può catalogare. Se le parole sono suoni articolati che simboleggiano e comunicano un'idea, il termine «mamma», a differenza di «mother», il nuovo termine acquisito, simboleggia e comunica un intero mondo di sentimenti che nessuna espressione straniera può comprendere e rispettare. Abolirlo

> significa rigettare l'esistenza di una fanciullezza intimamente legata a tutti gli episodi, piccoli e grandi, e a tutte le emozioni, importanti e non importanti, connessi ed ispirati da quell'unica parola. Non assimilazione o americanizazzione, dunque, ma ambivalenza, un'ambivalenza di pensiero e sentimento, di dubbio e di certezza, di sogno e realtà. (*La parola antica*, 143-144)[1]

La conseguenza di questa trasformazione è che l'immigrante, nell'esprimersi nella lingua acquisita, traduce non solo le parole ma anche il suo animo e in quel processo di traduzione lentamente e instancabilmente inizia a cambiare. Adesso lui/lei è in possesso della lingua e della cultura di due paesi: "America Italia; in quale ordine però! Non dovremmo dire: Italia America?" (*La parola antica*, 143). Tusiani si pone queste domande perché crede che l'immigrante non possa essere completamente assimilato nella cultura acquisita:

> Posta in termini diversi la domanda è: fino a qual punto l'emigrato può assimilare la nuova lingua e la nuova civiltà, e in che maniera dimenticare e rinnegare se stesso in mezzo alle nuove e impellenti esigenze della sua vita? Anche se la risposta sia priva di validità scientifica, il poeta ci dice che non esiste, e non può esistere, un assorbimento totale, e che non potrà mai esserci un'accettazione totale, cioè *spirituale*, delle tradizioni della nuova terra. (*La parola antica*, 143: enfasi mia)

Il continuo sentimento di "sradicamento" di Tusiani consiste soprattutto nel fatto che non si è mai integrato spiritualmente nella cultura americana. Questo

---

[1] Si veda anche "Song of the Bicentennial" in *Gente Mia and Other Poems*.

sentimento è espresso molto bene in "Song of the Bicentennial":

> Then who will solve this riddle of my day?
> Two languages, two lands, perhaps two souls . . .
> Am I a man or two strange halves of one?

E' precisamente questo indovinello insolto, e il sentimento di essere sospeso fra due mondi, di non appartenere, e di navigare fra due sistemi culturali che, penso, abbia spinto il Tusiani, dopo una lunga e meritoria carriera di poeta in lingua inglese e latina, a ritornare all'italiano per la sua autobiografia.

La soluzione dell'indovinello per il Tusiani consiste nel capire di essere un uomo di due mondi, nell' accettare il suo biculturalismo e di accettare se stesso come uomo di due lingue, due terre, e due anime. Dopo quarant'anni l'indovinello è sciolto. Le domande poste in "Song of the bicentennial" si sono trasformate in affermazioni.

Giovanni Cecchetti nato a Pescia in Toscana è emigrato negli subito dopo la seconda guerra mondiale, e mentre stava elaborando una poetica personale è diventato uno dei maggiori studiosi d'italianistica negli Stati Uniti. Nella sua lunga e insigne carriera ha diffuso gli studi italiani nei più prestigiosi atenei americani come la Stanford University e la University of California a Los Angeles (UCLA). Fra le sue pubblicazioni si trovano studi sul Leopardi, Verga e Pascoli; *La poesia del Pascoli*, *Leopardi e Verga*, *Il Verga maggiore*, *Giovanni Verga*; le sue traduzioni dall' italiano dei *Malavoglia e Mastro Don*

Gesualdo del Verga e le *Operette Morali/ Essays and Dialogues* del leopardi. Ha anche pubblicato raccolte di poesie, fra le quali *Diario nomade, Impossibile scendere, Nel cammino dei monti, Favole spente*; e tre volumi di prose, *Il villaggio degli inutili, Spuntature e intermezzi,* and *La danza nel deserto.*

Nonostante la sua lunga permanenza negli Stati Uniti, Cecchetti ha sempre scritto poesia e prosa in italiano; non per mancanza di abilità e conoscenza della lingua inglese – uno sguardo veloce ai suoi studi critici scritti in inglese dissipano qualunque dubbio, ma per via di una lealtà e devozione alla cultura italiana, e la sicurezza che l'unica vera poesia può essere scritta solamente nella lingua materna. In un breve saggio pubblicato nel 1992 su *Forum Italicum,* dal titolo "Sullo scriver poesia"Cecchetti scrive quanto segue:

> E la lingua? E' quella in cui si è nati; è la lingua d'un' infanzia trasfigurata, carica di quei sensi che allora sarebbero stati irragiungibili. Nessuno può scrivere poesia in un' altra lingua, sovrapposta e quindi fittizia, che non gli può diventare linguaggio, sebbene ci stia dentro quotidianamente. In questa può scrivere versi, magari dei buoni versi, ma non poesia la quale non può nascere in chi si trova bloccato nella prigione dell'artificio. Noi che abbiamo avuto un'infanzia in Italia (quell'infanzia che in certo modo include anche l'adolescenza) possiamo scrivere poesia solo in italiano. L'inglese è la lingua della prosa.

Le sue prime raccolte di poesie, *Diario nomade* (1967) e *Impossibile scendere* (1978) sono state discusse intelligentemente e favorevolmente da due studiosi anche loro emigrati nel Nord America – Fredi Chiappelli e Danilo Aguzzi-Barbaglia. Nei loro saggi,

Chiapelli e Aguzzi-Barbaglia hanno identificato l'esilio, la memoria, la inesorabilità del tempo, la battaglia esistenziale e spirituale dell'uomo moderno fra scenari e avvenimenti alienati e alienanti come gli elementi tematici più importanti nel lavoro di Cecchetti.[2]

Nella raccolta di racconti, *Danza nel deserto,* pubblicazta nel 1985, forae il suo lavoro migliore, sono ancora presenti tutti gli elementi tematici identificati dal Chiappelli e dall' Aguzzi-Barbaglia sono ancora presenti e rafforzati dall'uso del deserto californiano come palcoscenico e cornice per i dodici racconti che costituiscono questo volumetto.[3] Cecchetti ha vissuto sulla costa del pacifico e ai confini del deserto californiano per gli ultimi trent'anni. I racconti di *Danza nel deserto*, nell'echeggiare *Il deserto dei tartari* di Dino Buzzati, riflettono fortemente la lunga esperienza di vita e di lavoro di Cecchetti nel paesaggio americano. Il deserto per Cecchetti è la metafora della solitudine che avviluppa l'umanità nella società contemporanea e lo squallore che questa solitudine rappresenta. Nel deserto, la natura spezza i confini che noi consideriamo "normali," cioè quella normalità vivibile: sembra che "il deserto non comprenda l'uomo perché l'uomo non comprende il deserto." Con il deserto come palcoscenico e cornice questi racconti assumono toni e tinte surrealiste. Questi racconti dipingono un mondo fantastico, dove la realtà continuamente fluisce e si trasforma, pur sempre rimanendo realtà. Questi racconti, come

---

[2] Si veda la recensione di Rebecca West al *Cammino dei monti* (Firenze: Vallecchi, 1980) in *Forum Italicum* 15.1 (1981): 102.

[3] I racconti di *Danza nel deserto* sono: "Danza nel deserto," "Il telefono," "Il molo," "Il viale dei pirati," "La baia secca," "Le lettere," "Gl'ingessati," "Il castello," "Gl'ingabbiati," "Il cassone," "La macchina dell'aria," e "L'ascensore."

l'autore stesso ci dice in una intervista con Michele Lettieri, [4] non sono altro che "immagini del mondo in cui viviamo, quasi forme simboliche, ossia forme quasi allegoriche" (123). Gli uomini e le donne che popolano *Danza nel deserto* sono persone che esistono e agiscono in solitudine.

Quando cercano di rompere il muro della solitudine quello stesso muro diventa più solido e impenetrabile. *Danza nel deserto* è un libro sulla comunicazione, o meglio sulla mancanza di comunicazione nella società post-industriale:

> E' il mondo in cui vivo ancora: un mondo di gente che ride e che piange di là dalle vetrate, che muove serissima le labbra, senza che non ci sia mai un interlocutore. So che tutti cercano parole, dimentichi del nido del grillo canterino, e poi si contentano della risata solitaria o del sussurro di colomba.

Nel racconto "Il telefono," il viaggiatore/narratore di *Danza nel deserto* fa visita a un vecchio compagno di scuola che vive in una piccola casuccia di una stanza lontano dalla civiltà. Una volta entrato nella casa dell'amico il viaggiatore vede molti telefoni costruiti a forma di uomo e di donna:

> "Non capisco niente," dissi. M'avvicinai a un uomo con gli occhi tesi.
>
> "Non codesto. E' un ventriloquo. Ha il telefono in pancia; ripete solo quel che dicono i vicini." [...]
>
> "Prova a parlare con qualcuno," disse; "forse risponde ... Questo."

[4] Michael Lettieri. "*Danza nel deserto*: intervista a Giovanni Cecchetti." *Ipotesi 80* (giugno, 1989): 123-130.

> M'avvicinai e dissi nel ricevitore: "Come sta?" Mi giunse una risposta monosillabica, un suono agglutinato, come in cinese.
>
> Provai le altre statue; le risposte non cambiarono. A volte i suoni scivolavan via; a volte si gonfiavano in modo da sembrar grida disarticolate da giungla. M'arresi.
>
> "Senti," disse il vecchio compagno di scuola. "Credevo che con un estraneo diventassero normali. Invece ... Da principio cominciarono a farmi degli scherzi. Se dicevo qualcosa in un ricevitore, rispondevan con lunghi discorsi in coreano, in persiano, in armeno. . . o almeno così credevo, perché spesso non riuscivo nemmeno a riconoscer la lingua. ... Pensai che si fossero abituati a questi scherzi perché li avevo collegati alle linee internazionali. Allora li misi sulla rete nazionale. Peggio che peggio: colpi di tosse, abbai, grida, addirittura canzoncine a boccha chiusa. *Insomma voci, non parole....* C'è da disperarsi. (30-31)

I protagonisti di *Danza nel deserto* cercano di comunicare ma I loro tentativi sono costantemente vanificati, o dal loro stesso operare o da eventi che sono al di fuori della loro sfera di controllo. Vivono come in un mondo di sogni. La loro necessità di comunicare è così intensa che inventano modi di comunicare. E inventano modi di comunicare perché sono incapaci di comunicare, come nel caso, ci dice l'autore, dell' uomo contemporaneo in generale. Perché è diventato così difficile comunicare con il prossimo? Cecchetti dà una risposta nellastessa intervista citata:

> Il mondo che sognano, quello in cui poi finiscono per vivere, a volte è molto insolito, come è sempre il caso dei sogni; e quindi non è percepibile dagli altri. E' percepibile solo da loro stessi, perché gli altri hanno un loro mondo di sogni che è totalmente diverso. Questo spiega perché la

comunicazione è così difficile, anzi direi impossibile. E lo è naturalmente non solo per queste persone, ma per tutti gli altri che io non considero. (125)

L'impossibilità della comunicazione è il filo conduttore che lega le opere di Cecchetti. Ne *Il viaggio degli inutili*, opera giovanile ma di recente pubblicazione, il primo racconto, "La sporta del viandante" chiaramente esplora questo tema:

> Ogni tanto aprivo la sporta e ne tiravo fuori una casa o dei brandelli, e mi mettevo a studiarmeli in mano. Non mi ci volle molto ad accorgermi che nella sporta avevo creduto di metter l'infinito, ed invece non avevo depositato altro che una gran quantità di limiti. Continuai lo stesso a raccogliere e conservare. [...]
>
> Però troppe eran le cose che avevo e che dovevo portarmi dietro. Un giorno cominciai a tirar fuori quel che ci avevo messo, Ma tutto era incredibilmente cambiato. Ciò che era originariamente bianco s'era fatto rosso, e viceversa. Le cose azzurre eran diventategrigie. Ma che c'era dentro quella sporta per causare simili trasformazioni? Non l'ho mai saputo." (17-18)

Il deserto americano ritorna come protagonista ne *Il cammino dei monti*. Nella poesia dal titolo "Las Vegas" Cecchetti offre al lettore una delle esperienze più surrealistiche che si possa immaginare: Las Vegas, la città di metallo, neon e vetro che si alza dal deserto dell'ovest americano—*the city where America plays*. Messo davanti a questa immagine surrealistica l'agonia del poeta sul destino della società lo sopraffà:

> Mi rampolla negli orecchi la vertigine
> e cerco l'erba antica d'un presagio

Non ti sorprenda se barcollo sopra un filo di caligine
mentre da fondi fumosi frugo
mentre da fondi fumosi frugo.
Quasi fossi
sul punto di reimmergermi nel caos.

In un'aria di ruggine cascate
tintinnano nell'atrio, guizzano lumi, s'increspano
manubri — la polvere

intorpidisce le montagne nude. Allora
l'allucinato castello resiste
al bulino del vento e sogna
un naufragio di fango e di fiumi;

La città di Las Vegas è metafora della società contemporanea, una società priva di fondamenta, una società costruita sulla sabbia, destinata a crollare:

Se si stacca una scaglia ecco che crolla
a briciole la rete, e non c'è più nemmeno
un'ampolla opaca al chiodo
Della parete...

Il deserto, per Cecchetti, diventa metafora della nostra vita e della nostra società, e del vuoto incolmabile che è dentro tutti noi. L'uomo moderno, alla ricerca della felicità e della conoscenza, è caduto nell' abisso della disperazione e vede soltanto il deserto arido, inospitale e arido.

UNA CONCLUSIONE (PER MODO DI DIRE)

Come scrisse Paolo Valesio nella sua introduzione al libro *Italian Poets in America*, "Exile is a slinking beast; it bides its time, without hurry, but it gets you in the end. When all the illusions of moderation and equilibrium and normal routine are gone, we find ourselves face to face with a radical choice: ..." (5). L'individuo può accettare la sua condizione esistenziale di "altro" – di straniero, o può respingere questa condizione e cercare di inserirsi il più possibile nella sua nuova realtà e "with a constant policing of all his rebellious thoughts, doubts, or bursts of despair – live out his life as an adoptive existence." (Valesio, 5) I due poeti brevemente esaminati in questo saggio hanno affrontato il loro problema capitale in modi diversi. Tusiani è diventato poeta riconosciuto in lingua inglese e latina; affrontò la tragedia dell'emigrazione con i versi più belli e profondi visti negli annali della lettaraturaitalo-americana; e, ultimamente, è ritornato all'italiano e al dialetto della sua regione natia. Questo ritorno alla lingua madre (sia l'italiano che il dialetto) può essere interpretato come tentativo di soluzione al suo *stato* di uomo diviso fra due terre e due culture. Il problema per Tusiani è che quarant' anni di realtà americana non può essere cancellata e che questi anni hanno avuto un profondo effetto sulla sua vita e sul suo lavoro di poeta, traduttore e studioso. Nell'ultimo episodio della *Parola Antica*, ultimo volume della trilogia biografica, Tusiani racconta che ritornando dall'Italia, sogna di trovarsi con sua madre in un lungo corridoio illuminato da un'acceccante luce bianca con molte porte ai lati. All'inizio e alla fine del corridoio altre due porte con le scritte "Uscita" e l'altra "Entrata." Tusiani e la madre iniziano a camminare verso la porta marcata "Uscita." Quando arrivano in fondo si accorgono che adesso sulla porta c'è scritto "Entrata" e girandosi vedono che sulla porta opposta invece di "Entrata" c'è scritto "Uscita."

> Arrivai sotto quella scrittura e lessi «Entrata». Mi voltai e vidi, lì dov'era mia madre la parola «Uscita».... Rifeci il cammino, ma quando raggiunsi mia madre, in alto, al posto di «Uscita» lessi nuovamente «Entrata».... E per quaranta volte, affannato, ansioso, con la speranza e la disperazione che mi spingevano e guidavano, corsi da un'estremità all'altra di quell'enorme corridoio.... (308)

Quasi preso dal terrore, Tusiani nota le porte ai lati del corridoio e nota che su ogni porta c'è scritto il nome di una persona che ha avuto una forte influenza sulla sua vita. Bussa su ogni porta ma nessuno risponde. Finalmente, nella luce vede l'ombra di suo padre che morì alcuni anni prima:

> "Papà! Papà!" gli dissi, andandogli incontro, "ci siamo perduti io e mamma; non possiamo trovare l'uscita."
>
> "Sei proprio un bambino," mi rispose mio padre, sorridendo. "So io dov'è l'uscita: venite con me." Cominciavamo a seguirlo... (309)

A quel punto Tusiani viene svegliato dall'assistente di volo che annunciava l'arrivo a New York. Sembra che nessuno possa aiutare Tusaini a trovare l'"Uscita"; questo è un problema esistenziale al quale solo lui può trovare la risposta. Il libro, e l'autobiografia, finisce con questo piccolo paragrafo:

> Andando verso il Bronx, nella limousine della Poten (his brother's petroleum company), notai un altro particolare: i tergicristalli, strusciando da destra a sinistra, da sinistra a destra, sembravano dire Entrata-Uscita, Uscita-Entrata, ma non sapevo più che cosa significassero quelle due parole, né a chi fossero rivolte. (310)

Una lettura attenta di quest'ultimo paragrafo suggerisce che il Tusiani finalmente è arrivato ad una rsoluzione del suo problema di immigrato. La risoluzione è la consapevolezza di essere sospeso fra due mondi, riconoscere il suo biculturalismo e di accettare se stesso come uomo di due lingue e due anime socioculturali.

Per Cecchetti la strada è stata diversa. Tutta la sua attività di poeta e di scrittore in prosa si è svolta in italiano. I legami intimi di Cecchetti con la cultura italiana e con l'ovest americano fanno di lui una voce originale nella poesia degli ultimi trent'anni. I suoi continui attraversamenti del confine tra due culture danno vita a una letteratura che cattura "sia la natura effimera sia quella concreta di un mondo visto e di un'esperienza vissuta, che si concentra nello sforzo della coscienza umana tesa a spingersi oltre lo spazio e il tempo verso l'accettazione dei limiti di entrambi, una accettazione che potrebbe portare al rimpatrio dello spirito in esilio" (West, 98).

In questo saggio mi sono limitato a mettere in evidenza due dei sentieri intrapresi da scrittori italiani negli Stati Uniti.

Opere citate

Cecchetti, Giovanni. *Diario nomade.* Padova: Rebellato, 1967.

______. *Impossibile scendere.* Milano; Scheiwiller, 1978.

______. *Nel Cammino dei Monti.* Firenze: Vallecchi, 1981.

______. *Il villaggio degli inutili.* Venezia: Rebellato, 1981.

______. *Danza nel deserto.* Venezia: Rebellato, 1985.

Hicks, D. Emily. *Border Writing The Multidimensional Text.* U. Minnesota P., 1989.

Lettieri, Michael. "*Danza nel deserto*: intervista a Giovanni Cecchetti." *Ipotesi 80* (giugno, 1989): 123-130.

Pavese, Cesare. *Lettere.* Torino: Einaudi, 1968.

Tamburri, Anthony. Editor's Note to "Poessay VI: Voices from the Italian Diaspora." in *Romance Language Notes* II (1991): 13.

Tusiani, Joseph. *Gente Mia and Other Poems*. Stone PArk, IL: Italian Cultural Center, 1978.

_______. *La Parola Antica Autobiografia di un italo-americano*. Bari: Schena Editore, 1992.

_______. *La Parola Nuova Autobiografia di un italo-americano*. Bari: Schena Editore, 1991.

_______. *La Parola Difficile Autobiografia di un italo-americano*. Bari: Schena Editore, 1988

Valesio, Paolo. "Writer Between Two Worlds: Italian Writing in the United States Today." *Differentia* 3-4 (Spring/ Autumn 1989): 259-276.

_______. Introduction to *Italian Poets in America* (1993): 5-8.

Valesio, Paolo and Peter Carravetta, eds. *Poesaggio*. Quinto di Treviso: Pagus editore, 1993.

Viscusi, Robert. "*De vulgari eloquentia*: An Approach to the Language of Italian American Fiction." *Yale Italian Studies*, I.3 (1981): 21-38.

West, Rebecca. Review of Cecchetti's *Cammino dei monti* (Firenze: Vallecchi, 1980) in *Forum Italicum* 15.1 (1981): 102.

Gli americani italiani ed il cinema[1]

Anthony Julian Tamburri
John D. Calandra Italian American Institute
Queens College/CUNY

Uno sguardo alla storia degli italiani ed americani italiani nei tre principali media rivela immediatamente che gli italiani e gli americani italiani non sono affatto una minoranza in cinema, musica, e televisione; né lo sono mai stati in termini di presenza effettiva o semplicemente di rappresentazione in film di non americani italiani. Fin dall'avvento di queste tre principali arene culturali gli americani italiani sono sempre stati visibili. Basti pensare a Rudolph Valentino, Madonna, o Ezio Pinza per rendersi conto che gli americani italiani hanno sempre goduto di ampia visibilità, per quanto a volte discutibile, in film, video musicali e in TV. I dibattiti a tal proposito imperversano infatti da anni e, pur abbracciando la causa dell'anti-diffamazione italiana, é possibile af-

[1] Malgrado ci sia ancora in Italia l'usanza di chiamare gli Americani di origine italiana "italoamericani", termine alquanto problematico e – solo a riguardo della denominazione – piuttosto discusso. Io, da parte mia, avevo già optato in inglese per il termine "Italian American" come sostantivo e "Italian/American" come aggettivo, i quali in lingua italiana andrebbero tradotti "Italiano Americano" per il sostantivo e, ciò che alcuni riterrebbero un mostriciattolo di appellativo, "Italiano/Americano" per la forma aggettivale. Ciononostante, in questa sede con la stessa nozione che ha motivato l'uso della mia nomenclatura inglese, adoperando come aggettivo il binomio con la barra, e come sostantivo il termine senza, farò delle piccole modifche in modo che il binomio in italiano segua anche lo spirito della grammatica italiana, per cui specialmente per il sostantivo, adopero il binomio "Americano Italiano" per l'equivalente dell'inglese "Italian American", dato che il sostantivo indica l'attuale località di esistenza mentre l'aggettivo segnala l'eredità culturale.

Per l'uso della barra (/) al posto del trattino (-), vedere il mio saggio *To Hyphenate Or Not To Hyphenate. The Italian/American Writer: An* Other *American* (Montreal: Guernica Editions, 1991).

frontarli da diversi punti di vista. Una prospettiva monolitica puó infatti rivelarsi controproducente per avanzare il dibattito, o perlomeno per mitigarne i toni, come sottolinea Jonathan Cavallero quando osserva che:

> negli ultimi anni gruppi quali la American Italian Defense Association e la National Italian American Foundation hanno protestato contro la rappresentazione degli italiani nella serie TV – prodotta da HBO - *The Sopranos* (dal 1999 a oggi), ignorando invece rappresentazioni più recenti degli italiani e persino applaudendo pubblicità televisive come quella per Ragu, o quella radiofonica per Sprint PCS, e la serie *Friends* – prodotta da NBC (1994- presente). Tali scelte indicano come questi gruppi applichino un doppio standard, discriminando i gangster, ma trascurando altre forme di stereotipo.[2]

Potremmo infatti criticare alcuni dei film e programmi TV "italiano/americani" più seguiti che popolano il piccolo e grande schermo e riscuotono un alto indice di gradimento tra gli stessi americani italiani. Tra questi, Cavallero ricorda giustamente il programma *Friends*, il cui unico personaggio italiano/americano non costituisce certamente un modello ideale a cui aspirare. Simili critiche potrebbero essere mosse al sempre popolare *Everybody Loves Raymond*, dove madre e padre insieme ai due figli fanno fare agli americani italiani la parte – per mantenerci nei termini intuitivi di Cavallero – dei buffoni e dei fessi.[3]

[2] Vedere il suo "Gangsters, Fessos, Tricksters, and Sopranos: the Historical Roots of Italian American Stereotype Anxiety," *Journal of Popular Film and Television* (Summer 2004): 50-1.

[3] Vorrei ricordare al lettore un altro personaggio televisivo ignorato dalla maggioranza della comunità italiano/americana, Jason Alexander e il suo personaggio socialmente disadattato, George Costanza, in *Seinfeld*.

La colpa, tuttavia, se di colpa si può parlare, non é da attribuirsi esclusivamente ai produttori ed attori di questi film e programmi televisivi, bensì anche - e potremmo sostenere in ugual misura - al pubblico italiano e italiano/americano e all' intellighenzia italiana ed italiano/americana. Spetta infatti a questo secondo gruppo - ossia i mediatori culturali dell' America italiana - il dovere di articolare un discorso ben documentato, rigoroso, che esplori e critichi tutti i punti di vista con rispetto, attenzione e serietà, in termini a tutti comprensibili. Tale compito é fondamentale affinché gli americani italiani formino un gruppo unito - che includa tutti gli americani italiani - e delineino una strategia retorica che, come Robert Viscusi ha già eloquentemente osservato, costruisca una volta per tutte una narrativa di gruppo.[4] Ciò significa includere anche i cosiddetti "blasfematori" dell'America italiana quali Francis Ford Coppola e Martin Scorsese, o Mario Puzo, Al Pacino, e Robert DeNiro, per menzionare solo alcuni di coloro che sembrano essere stati relegati ai margini dell'America italiana benpensante dai suoi principali interlocutori.[5]

Negli ultimi dieci anni in particolare il ritratto negativo degli americani italiani ha irritato una discreta percentuale di questo gruppo etnico, ma esso ha le sue origini agli inizi del ventesimo secolo con l'avvento del sonoro, se non addirittura prima. Film muti quali *The Black Hand* (1906) di Edwin Porter e

[4] Vedere l'eccellente saggio di Viscusi, "Breaking the Silence: Strategic Imperatives for Italian American Culture," *Voices in Italian Americana* 1.1 (1990): 1-13.

[5] Per una discussione sulla nozione di una visione più inclusiva degli studi italiano/americani, vedere il mio studio *A Semiotic of Ethnicity: In (Re)cognition of the Italian/American Writer* (Albany: SUNY P, 1998), specificatamente il capitolo 8.

The Avenging Conscious (1914) di D. W. Griffith possono infatti considerarsi come *buone* e precoci fonti di tale stereotipizzazione. Non a caso in questi film il personaggio italiano/americano è un ricattatore di cattiva fama impersonato da attori non italiano/americani, come era spesso il caso all'epoca.[6] Temi quali il sesso, la violenza, il sentimentalismo, la famiglia e simili hanno finito per dominare il cinema sugli americani italiani e dei registi italiano/americani. Tale tendenza ha cosí provocato un acceso dibattito nella comunità italiano/americana alla fine del ventesimo secolo sulle rappresentazioni degli italiani o americani italiani nei media statunitensi. Già col suo precedente film, *At The Altar* (1909), Griffith aveva infatti suscitato preoccupazione nella cultura dominante, quando, in un segmento narrativo apparentemente positivo, aveva insistito su sessualità e violenza come aspetti tipici del carattere italiano. In effetti, aggressività e sessualità diventeranno caratteristiche comuni dei personaggi italiani ed italiano/americani nel cinema statunitense a venire. Fondendo l'immagine del gangster violento, che ha le sue origini nei film gangster degli anni trenta, e i personaggi ipersessuati degli anni successivi, il maschio italiano culminerà infatti nella figura di Tony Soprano, un capofamiglia mafioso violento e ipersessuato che arriva quasi al punto di sedurre la fidanzata del proprio nipote, Adriana.

Durante i primi anni del cinema statunitense, gli italiani e gli americani italiani furono impersonati

---

[6] Per un'attenta lettura della rappresentazione dell'italiano in questo primo periodo nel cinema statunitense, vedere l'eccellente studio di Ilaria Serra *Immagini di un Immaginario: L"emigrazione Italiana negli Stati Uniti fra I Due Secoli (1890-1924)* (Verona, Italy: CIERRE, 1997), in particolare pp. 102-59.

soprattutto da non italiani o non americani italiani. *The Italian* (1914) di Thomas Ince e Reginald Baker é sicuramente considerato uno dei capolavori dell'era del muto. Attento alle sventure dell'immigrato, il film racconta le prove e tribolazioni di Beppe Donnetti (rappresentato da George Beban) e la sua vana ricerca di successo e benessere negli Stati Uniti. Confinato nel ghetto degli immigrati da cui ha cercato di evadere per tutta una vita, Donnetti sarà condannato a guardare passivamente il proprio figlio soccombere alla malattia.[7]

Bisogna aspettare l'arrivo di Rudolph Valentino per vedere un attore italiano in un ruolo da protagonista sul grande schermo, anche se va notato che raramente Valentino ha impersonato un italiano in un ruolo centrale. *The Four Horsemen of the Apocalypse* (1921) e *The Sheik* (1921) furono i suoi trampolini di lancio e rimangono ancora oggi i suoi film più noti. Attore italiano di bell'apparenza e fama internazionale, Valentino fu uno dei primi sex symbol del grande schermo. Esotici, ribelli e ricchi di carica sessuale, così erano i suoi personaggi, e per questo, come ha ben osservato John Paul Russo (227), l'attore Valentino ha probabilmente "incarnato l'archetipo dell'italiano nella psiche popolare [statunitense e non italiana]."[8]

Sul modello di *Little Caesar* (1930) di Mervyn Leroy, gli americani italiani sullo schermo continuarono ad essere impersonati da non italiani fino agli

---

[7] Per un'eccellente analisi di questo film, rimando nuovamente allo studio di Serra, *Immagini di un Immaginario* (137-55),.

[8] Non va certo persa l'ironia per cui la carriera di Valentino fu di fatto lanciata per cosi dire a scapito di un altro gruppo di 'altri.' Benché non impersonasse italiani sullo schermo, Valentino rappresentò sempre maschi esotici, in particolare il maschio arabo, per cosi dire l'altro lato del maschio mediterraneo.

anni trenta e quaranta.[9] In quello stesso periodo, tuttavia, molti registi di origine italiana lavoravano giá assiduamente negli Stati Uniti, benché fossero pochi i film che si occupavano degli italiani in America. Erano infatti gli anni di Frank Capra e Vincent Minnelli, due dei registi più prolifici e affermati nella prima metà del ventesimo secolo. I loro film, tuttavia, presentavano raramente personaggi italiani o italiano/americani, e proprio quest'assenza potrebbe spiegare il loro successo. Decidendo di non soffermarsi sul loro patrimonio etnico, evitarono forse di trattare questioni che il pubblico dell'epoca preferiva ignorare, come le lotte degli immigrati proletari o della loro prole. All'epoca erano i film a lieto fine e i musical a riscuotere il maggior successo di pubblico e ad avere la meglio su tematiche incentrate sulle tribolazioni del proletariato. Si possono cercare personaggi italiani in ruoli secondari nei loro film, ma se ne trovano raramente; il più noto é probabilmente il signor Martini in *It's a Wonderful Life*. Una rara eccezione, é, invece, *A Hole in the Head* di Capra, il suo cinquantaduesimo film e ciononostante il primo interamente basato su personaggi e tematiche italiano/americane.[10]

Perché gli americani italiani diventino attori principali nell'industria cinematografica – sullo schermo o dietro la cinepresa – dovremo aspettare ancora alcuni anni. Alla fine degli anni quaranta, per esempio,

---

[9] A tal proposito, si può osservare una certa ironia in quanto quindici anni dopo Mervyn Leroy dirigerà un piccolo film, *The House I live In* (1945), con Frank Sinatra che tratta della persecuzione religiosa, di questioni non lontane a dir la verità dalla stereotipizzazione etnica. Vedere il mio "Frank Sinatra and Notions of 'Tolerance': *The House I Live In*" (in pubblicazione) per ulteriori informazioni.

[10] Per una lettura dettagliata di questo film, vedere l'eccellente saggio di John Paul Russo, "An Unacknowledged Masterpiece: Capra's Italian-American Film," *Screening Ethnicity*, 291-321.

Richard Conte ottiene un ruolo non da gangster e l'attrice Ida Lupino comincia la sua carriera cinematografica, scrivendo e dirigendo cinque film tra il 1949 e il 1953, per poi dedicarsi al lavoro di regista anche in televisione. Si dovranno, invece, aspettare gli anni sessanta e l'avvento di una mentalità più aperta nei confronti delle questioni etniche, perché giovani registi quali Michael Cimino, Francis Ford Coppola, Brian DePalma, Penny Marshall e Martin Scorsese, per menzionare solo i più rinomati, lascino il segno e spianino la strada per i successivi Greg Mottola, Nancy Savoca, Nick Stagliano, Sylvester Stallone, e Stanley Tucci.

Al di là dell'eccellente regia di questo gruppo di "nuovi" registi hollywoodiani e dei loro successori, va notato che i loro film affrontano una grande varietà di tematiche. Ritroviamo il tanto dibattuto tema della mafia in Coppola (*Godfather I & II* [1972/1974]) e Scorsese (*Mean Streets* [1973]), trasformato poi in un'attenzione generica al crimine organizzato – se non addirittura di piccole città – nei film di De Palma (*Scarface* [1983]), Stallone (*Paradise Alley* [1978]) e Stagliano (*The Florentine* [1999]). Dall'onnipotente "padrino" al "piccolo delinquente" di quartiere, il tema della mafia ha certamente lasciato il segno nell' immaginario americano relativamente agli americani italiani. Per quanto molto contestata, infatti, l'immagine dell'americano italiano mafioso è innegabilmente anche molto popolare. Non si può quindi escludere la possibilità che più che un semplice criminale questa figura sia diventata in qualche modo un'icona contro-culturale, simbolo di colui che dai bassifondi riesce a emergere e a "battere il sistema," benché il sistema sia una cosiddetta struttura sociale legittima.[11] Così pare che sia stato interpretato *The Godfather* di Puzo e Coppola,[12] il prototipo del gangster moderno, dove Don Corleone batte il sistema, o perlomeno così sembra. Coppola con il suo film ha infatti creato una perfetta strategia retorica che permette questa lettura primaria. A questo proposito, Marco Greco ha già notato "l'idiozia dei discorsi su pasta e mafiosi" che gli americani considerano come caratteristiche italiane per eccellenza.[13] Sulla scia del lavoro di Gardaphè sulle affinitá tra la figura del gangster e del cowboy, potremmo affermare che film quali *The Godfather* (1972), *Mean Streets* (1973), e/o *GoodFellas* (1989) richiedono una lettura più attenta che permetta di cogliere le strutture semiotiche profonde del testo. Relativamente ai tre film suddetti, non dobbiamo dimenticare che il gangster fu unanimemente presentato come un individuo violento fisicamente, e spesso privo di sentimenti, *in nuce* un essere umano meschino e spregevole.

---

[11] In riferimento agli italiani, non dovremmo dimenticare quel fatalismo tipico degli italiani del sud che accompagnò l'immigrante dall'Italia agli Stati Uniti, in particolare durante i primi quarant'anni dell'emigrazione italiana. Oltre ad esempi di tale scetticismo e fatalismo riscontrabili in alcuni dei primi romanzi – e a questo riguardo vorrei sottolineare *Christ in Concrete* (1939) – è interessante notare anche *Cristo si é fermato ad Eboli* di Carlo Levi (1943). Il romanzo costituisce infatti un perfetto esempio di come il cosiddetto sistema legittimo sia visto come uno dei mali necessari che il genere umano deve affrontare al pari di disastri naturali, tempeste, malaria e altre malattie o istituzioni come la Chiesa, Roma e altre istituzioni sociali.

[12] Altri due saggi che includerei tra le letture "obbligatorie" in merito a *The Godfather* sono: Thomas J. Ferraro, "Blood in the Marketplace: The Business of Family in *The Godfather* Narratives," *Ethnic Passages: Literary Immigrants in Twentieth-Century America* (Chicago: U Chicago P, 1993) 18-52, e Marianna De Marco Torgovnick, "*The Godfather* as the World's Most Typical Novel," *Crossing Ocean Parkway: Readings by an Italian American Daughter* (Chicago, U Chicago P, 1994) 109-36.

[13] Vedere la sua intervista nel documentario di Will Parriniello *Little Italy* (1995).

A tal proposito vorrei portare semplicemente l'esempio della morte di Don Vito in *The Godfather*. Giocando con il nipote Anthony, Don Vito finge di essere un mostro. A parte l'iniziale paura che il nonno suscita in Anthony, significativa di per sé, altri due elementi sono degni di nota: 1) l'immagine di Don Corleone che corre tra le piante di pomodoro e passa dal ruolo di inseguitore a quello di inseguito é l'ultima che abbiamo di lui 2) mentre giace a terra morente, l'ignaro nipote Anthony comincia a spruzzare sul nonno quello che potremmo ritenere un insetticida, se non persino DDT considerati gli anni in questione. Una tale combinazione di eventi é troppo significativa per essere ignorata, quasi un simbolo del distacco della futura generazione – rappresentata qui da Anthony – dal vecchio mondo del crimine organizzato.[14] Inoltre, non dobbiamo dimenticare che proprio nelle scene successive Michael dimostra d'essersi trasformato in una persona fredda e spietata. Seguono infatti le scene intrecciate dei cinque omicidi da lui commissionati e del battesimo in cui Michael fa da padrino al figlio della sorella, la quale presto rimarrà vedova per mano dello stesso fratello.[15] Un individuo così spregevole non dovrebbe certo venir dipinto sotto una luce positiva in quello che possiamo considerare il cinema italiano/americano. Come notato precedentemente, spesso questo aspetto biasimevole dei mafiosi viene invece messo in

[14] In retrospettiva naturalmente, la scena si dimostra molto ironica e si distingue dalle altre alla luce di *The Godfather III*, dove diventa chiaro che Anthony si é completamente distanziato dagli affari di famiglia per seguire i propri interessi, cioè cantare all'opera, incurante del disaccordo del padre.

[15] Vorrei qui brevemente far notare la cravatta di Michael. Nel corso di *The Godfather* Michael indossa sempre la stessa cravatta, a strisce nere, bianche e grigie che ricorda troppo la tipica cravatta da direttore delle pompe funebri per essere una casuale coincidenza.

primo piano, una sorta di censura che si manifesta in una forma ironica di bullismo estetico, quando la presenza di personaggi mafiosi viene considerata assolutamente necessaria ai fini narrativi.

Con la seconda ondata di registi italiano/americani, il tema mafioso comincia a scemare, lasciando spazio ad altre questioni apparentemente più immediate per il repertorio estetico di questi giovani registi. Veniamo quindi fatti partecipi di affari di famiglia e questioni di genere nei film di Marshall, Mottola, Savoca, Tucci, ed altri. Le difficoltà della classe lavoratrice e delle giovani donne, per esempio, sono al centro della prima regia di Penny Marshall, mentre *Daytrippers* (1996) di Greg Mottola esamina le relazioni coniugali tra americani italiani all'interno della famiglia. Nancy Savoca e Stanley Tucci, invece, affrontano di petto la loro identità italiano/americana. In *True Love* (1989) e *Household Saints* (1993) Savoca interroga i valori del vecchio mondo e della comunità italiano/americana e tutto ciò che essa rappresenta (in riferimento a genere, lavoro, noi vs. loro).[16] Tucci, dal canto suo, esplora le prove e tribolazioni dei nuovi immigrati, nel co-diretto *Big Night* (1995), la storia di due fratelli che cercano di integrarsi negli Stati Uniti del dopoguerra.[17]

Tra i nuovissimi artisti già autori di almeno un lungometraggio vanno menzionati Tom DeCerchio

---

[16] Per ulteriori analisi dei film della Savoca, vedere i seguenti testi: Edvige Giunta, "The Quest for True Love: Ethnicity in Nancy Savoca's Domestic Film Comedy," *Screening Ethnicity*, 259-75; Gloria Nardini, "Is it *True Love*? or Not? Patterns of Ethnicity and Gender in Nancy Savoca." *Voices in Italian Americana* 2.1 (Spring 1991): 9-17; Edvige Giunta, "Narratives of Loss: Voices of Ethnicity in Agnes Rossi and Nancy Savoca." Special Issue on Italian American Culture. *Canadian Journal of Italian Studies* 19 (1996): 164-83.

[17] Per ulteriori informazioni su Stanley Tucci, vedere Anna Camaiti Hostert, "Big Night, Small Days," *Screening Ethnicity*, 249-58,.

(*Celtic Pride* [1996]), Helen De Michiel (*Tarantella* [1995]), Tony Piccirillo (*The 24th Day* [2004]) e Marylou Tibaldo-Bongiorno (*Little Kings* [2003]). Mentre tra i registi di cortometraggi, ricordiamo MariaRosy Calleri, Joe Greco, e Kim Ragusa. Dopo un debutto da *tour de force* con il cortometraggio, *Nunzio's Second Cousin* (1994),[18] DeCerchio arriva sul grande schermo con *Celtic Pride,* un film che esplora gli eccessi del fanatismo tra il proletariato. *The 24th Day* di Piccirillo, invece, é un thriller psicologico che affronta il tema della responsabilità individuale per le proprie azioni. De Michiel e Tibaldo-Bongiorno, a loro volta, mettono in primo piano la loro identità italiano/americana: *Tarantella* narra il ritorno di una giovane donna in occasione del funerale della madre e racconta l'emozionante riscoperta della sua eredità italiana. *Little Kings,* dal canto suo, esamina il rapporto tra tre fratelli nonché le loro relazioni con le varie donne della loro vita. Tutti e quattro i registi presentano una certa nuova visione del mondo per la nuova generazione di americani italiani . Nonostante il "mafioso" sia ancora presente in film recenti quali *Federal Hill* (1994) di Michael Corrente, in questa nuova generazione riscontriamo soprattutto la voglia di affrontare questioni come genere, sessualità, classe sociale, ed etnicità in maniera più approfondita, una *ars rhetorica* che è nuova alla regia italiano/americana.

Alcuni dei suddetti registi si sono cimentati anche nel genere documentaristico. Il primo a venire in mente è sicuramente *Italianamerican* (1974) di Scor-

[18] Per una dettagliata analisi testuale del cortometraggio di DeCerchio, *Nunzio's Second Cousin,* vedere il mio studio *Italian/American Short Films & Videos: A Semiotic Reading: A Semiotic Reading* (West Lafayette: Purdue UP, 2002) 29-52.

sese, dove, durante una visita pomeridiana che sembra una cena domenicale, il regista italiano/americano fa sedere i propri genitori davanti alla cinepresa e fa raccontare loro le esperienze e l'infanzia da figli di immigrati nella Little Italy di New York. Scorsese ci offre qui un intreccio dei racconti di Charles e Catherine con alcuni inserti storici che aiutano a dare un senso di autenticità ad un aspetto dell'America italiana. Tra i registi della nuova generazione anche Tibaldo-Bongiorno, Calleri e Ragusa hanno diretto documentari. *Mother-Tongue: Italian American Sons & Mothers* (1999) di Tibaldo-Bongiorno mostra come un gruppo di sette americani italiani si relaziona con le proprie madri, e tra gli intervistati troviamo Martin Scorsese, John Turturro, e Rudy Giuliani. Calleri, invece, offre un documentario unico e "sperimentale" che discute contemporaneamente questioni di genere, razza ed etnicità articolate tramite una serie di voci fuori campo e canzoni extradiegetiche. Una nota di merito nel genere documentaristico va certo a Tony DeNonno che ha dedicato la sua decennale carriera soprattutto a questo genere, vincendo anche una serie di premi. Da *Part of Your Loving* (1977) al più recente *Heaven Touches Brooklyn in July* (2004), DeNonno ha catturato le molte sfaccettature dell'America italiana, in particolare nelle sue forme quotidiane dell'america nord-orientale.

Per quanto si possa oggi sostenere che le rappresentazioni negative degli italiani ed americani italiani si siano mitigate grazie alla nuova sensibilità etnica che ha le sue origini nel movimento dei diritti civili degli anni sessanta e nello straordinario successo della serie televisiva *Roots* nella metà degli anni settanta, tale posizione può essere contestata facilmente rimandando ad alcuni film di Coppola e Scorsese – in particolare *GoodFellas* (1989) e *The Godfather III* (1990) - e più recentemente a rappresentazioni tipo *The Sopranos* (1999-).

Il sito internet "Italians (Includes Sicilians)" elenca un totale di 209 programmi televisivi in cui italiani ed americani italiani sono apparsi in ruoli principali o secondari. Come per il cinema e i video musicali, le opportunità sembrano innumerevoli e le apparizioni frequenti, ma é il tipo di rappresentazione che, a ragione, preoccupa maggiormente oggi. Considerata l'era della politica identitaria in cui ci troviamo dopo aver superato la soglia del ventunesimo secolo, emergono numerosi interrogativi sulla questione etnica, tra cui innanzitutto: chi ha il diritto di rappresentare un'etnia e quali sono i confini da non superare, se ve ne sono? La sentenza, potremmo dire, è ancora sospesa, come lo é in merito al grado di validità di tali argomenti, in quanto si potrebbe sempre far ricorso al vecchio adagio che una "cattiva" pubblicità é sempre meglio di nessuna pubblicità, alimentando così ulteriormente il dibattito in corso.

Contributors

Fred Gardaphé directs the Italian American Studies Program at the State University of New York at Stony Brook. His publications include: *Italian Signs, American Streets: The Evolution of Italian American Narrative* (1996), named an Outstanding Academic Book for 1996 by Choice, *Moustache Pete is Dead!* (1998), *Leaving Little Italy: Essaying Italian American Culture* (2004), and *From Wiseguys to Wise Men: The Gangster and Italian American Masculinities* (2006).

Paolo A. Giordano is chair of Modern Languages and Literatures at the University of Central Florida. A scholar of Renaissance and 20th-Century Italian Literature and Italian-American Literature, who has published widely on both fields, his publications include: "Gabriello Chiabrera", *Dictionary of Literary Biographies* (forthcoming); *Esilio migrazione e sogno Americano* (2002); *L'esilio come certezza* (1998); and *Beyond the Margin: Further Writings in Italian Americana* (1998).

Anthony Julian Tamburri is Dean of the John D. Calandra Italian American Institute of Queens College/CUNY. His publications include: *A Semiotic of Ethnicity: In (Re)cognition of the Italian/American Writer* (1998); *Italian/American Short Films & Videos: A Semiotic Reading.* (2002); and *Semiotics of Re-reading: Guido Gozzano, Aldo Palazzeschi, and Italo Calvino* (2003), published in Italy as *Una semiotica della ri-lettura: Guido Gozzano, Aldo Palazzeschi, e Italo Calvino* (2003), and *Narrare altrove: ovvero diverse segnalature letterarie* (2006).

Gardaphé, Giordano, and Tamburri co-direct Bordighera Press, an imprint of Bordighera Incorporated (which they founded in 1989) and publisher of the semi-annual, *Voices in Italian Americana.*

www.bordigherapress.org

VIA FOLIOS

A refereed book series dedicated to Italian studies and the culture of Italian Americans in North America.

EMANUEL CARNEVALI
Furnished Rooms
Vol. 43, forthcoming

ANTHONY ELLIS, ET AL.
Shifting Borders Negotiating Places
Vol. 42, Interdisciplinary Studies, $18.00

GEORGE GUIDA
Low Italian
Vol. 41, Poetry, forthcoming

FRED GARDAPHÈ, PAOLO GIORDANO, ANTHONY JULIAN TAMBURRI
Introducing Italian Americana: Generalities on Literature and Fim
Vol. 40, Italian American Studies, $10.00

DANIELA GIOSEFFI
Blood Autumn/Autunno di sangue
Vol. 39, Poetry, $15.00

FRED MISURELLA
Lies to Live by
Vol. 38, Stories, $15.00

STEVEN BELLUSCIO
Constructing a Bibliography
Vol. 37

ANTHONY JULIAN TAMBURRI, ED.
Italian Cultural Studies 2002
Vol. 36, Essays, $18.00

BEA TUSIANI
con amore
Vol. 35, Memoir, $19.00

FLAVIA BRIZIO-SKOV, ED.
Reconstructing Societies in the Aftermath of War
Vol. 34, History/Cultural Stud., $30.00

A.J. TAMBURRI, M.S. RUTHENBERG, G. PARATI, AND B. LAWTON, EDS.
Italian Cultural Studies 2001
Vol. 33, Essays, $18.00

ELIZABETH GIOVANNA MESSINA, ED.
In Our Own Voices
Vol. 32, Ital. Amer. Studies, $25.00

STANISLAO G. PUGLIESE
Desperate Inscriptions
Vol. 31, History, $12.00

ANNA CAMAITI HOSTERT & ANTHONY JULIAN TAMBURRI, EDS.
Screening Ethnicity
Vol. 30, Ital. Amer. Culture, $25.00

G. PARATI & B. LAWTON, EDS.
Italian Cultural Studies
Vol. 29, Essays, $18.00

HELEN BAROLINI
More Italian Hours & Other Stories
Vol. 28, Fiction, $16.00

FRANCO NASI, A CURA DI
Intorno alla Via Emilia
Vol. 27, Culture, $16.00

ARTHUR L. CLEMENTS
The Book of Madness and Love
Vol. 26, Poetry, $10.00

JOHN CASEY, ET. AL
Imagining Humanity
Immagini dell'umanità
Vol. 25, Interdisciplinary Studies, $18.00

ROBERT LIMA
Sardinia • Sardegna
Vol. 24, Poetry, $10.00

DANIELA GIOSEFFI
Going On
Vol. 23, Poetry, $10.00

ROSS TALARICO
The Journey Home
Vol. 22, Poetry, $12.00

EMANUEL DI PASQUALE
The Silver Lake Love Poems
Vol. 21, Poetry, $7.00

JOSEPH TUSIANI
Ethnicity
Vol. 20, Selected Poetry, $12.00

JENNIFER LAGIER
Second Class Citizen
Vol. 19, Poetry, $8.00

FELIX STEFANILE
The Country of Absence
Vol. 18, Poetry, $9.00

PHILIP CANNISTRARO
Blackshirts
Vol. 17, History, $12.00

LUIGI RUSTICHELLI, ED.
Seminario sul racconto
Vol. 16, Narrativa, $10.00

LEWIS TURCO
Shaking the Family Tree
Vol. 15, Poetry, $9.00

LUIGI RUSTICHELLI, ED.
Seminario sulla drammaturgia
Vol. 14, Theater/Essays, $10.00

Fred L. Gardaphè
Moustache Pete is Dead!
Long Live Moustache Pete!
Vol. 13, Oral literature, $10.00

JONE GAILLARD CORSI
Il libretto d'autore, 1860–1930
Vol. 12, Criticism, $17.00

HELEN BAROLINI
Chiaroscuro: Essays of Identity
Vol. 11, Essays, $15.00

T. PICARAZZI AND W. FEINSTEIN, EDS.
An African Harlequin in Milan
Vol. 10, Theater/Essays, $15.00

JOSEPH RICAPITO
Florentine Streets and Other Poems
Vol. 9, Poetry, $9.00

FRED MISURELLA
Short Time
Vol. 8, Novella, $7.00

NED CONDINI
Quartettsatz
Vol. 7, Poetry, $7.00

ANTHONY JULIAN TAMBURRI, ED.
MARY JO BONA, INTROD.
Fuori: Essays by Italian/American Lesbians and Gays
Vol. 6, Essays, $10.00

ANTONIO GRAMSCI
PASQUALE VERDICCHIO,
TRANS. & INTROD.
The Southern Question
Vol. 5, Social Criticism, $5.00

DANIELA GIOSEFFI
Word Wounds and Water Flowers
Vol. 4, Poetry, $8.00

WILEY FEINSTEIN
Humility's Deceit: Calvino Reading Ariosto Reading Calvino
Vol. 3, Criticism, $10.00

PAOLO A. GIORDANO, ED.
Joseph Tusiani: Poet, Translator, Humanist
Vol. 2, Criticism, $25.00

ROBERT VISCUSI
Oration Upon the Most Recent Death of Christopher Columbus
Vol. 1, Poetry, $3.00

Published by BORDIGHERA, INC., an independently owned not-for-profit scholarly organization that has no legal affiliation to the University of Central Florida, The John D. Calandra Italian American Institute, or State University of New York—Stony Brook.

www.ingramcontent.com/pod-product-compliance
Lightning Source LLC
LaVergne TN
LVHW050936080826
845145LV00004B/1287

* 9 7 8 1 8 8 4 4 1 9 8 0 5 *